Marie's Journey of Love

Marie Mohr-Grandstaff

Marie's Journey of Love

Marie Mohr-Grandstaff

Copyright 2014
By Marie Mohr-Grandstaff

First printing: April 2014

All Rights Reserved.
No part of this book may be reproduced, stored in a retrieval system, or transmitted by any means, electronic, mechanical, photocopying, recording, or otherwise, without written permission from the publisher.

ISBN: 978-1-939625-85-4
Library of Congress Control Number: 2013900640

Published by Inkwell Productions
10869 N. Scottsdale Road # 103-128
Scottsdale, AZ 85254-5280

Tel. 480-315-3781
E-mail info@inkwellproductions.com
Website www.inkwellproductions.com

Printed in the United States of America

Dedication

This book is dedicated with love and peace to my dear parents, who brought me into this world. They gave me the gift of life. They encouraged and walked with me on the journey of love. Their love made it all possible.

I dedicate it also to my sisters, brothers, grandparents, and extended family, plus my International Grail family, The Harp Foundation family, and my many friends around the world.

Dear Lord, inspire me, and may the angels guide me.

Marie's Journey of Love

Acknowledgments

I wish to acknowledge three special friends, connected with The Harp Foundation: Joyce Buekers, Susan Seats, and Lesa-Caldarella-Wong. They urged me to get my life story in print, took my journals and articles, and helped with editing, proofreading, poetry and harp photographs. Years ago my father plus, some of my family, encouraged me to write our story.

My deepest gratitude to my friends Linda Goad and Barbara Holden, who typed some sections.

The recent and final push came from Nick Ligidakis, my publisher. My dear soul-sister, Dr. Gladys McGarey, introduced me to Nick.

Thanks for the blessed opportunity to see this, my story, unfold.

Marie Mohr-Grandstaff and Dr. Gladys McGarey

Marie's Journey of Love

Marie's Journey of Love

Notes from Marie

Well, believe it or not, here I am after all these years, finally sitting down with my friends to record the precious memories of my past. Over the years, many people, especially friends and family, have told me I should share my incredible experiences and unusual adventures. My life has been so varied that it's almost been like living several lifetimes. Here is my hope for all of you reading this: may my spirit guide my thoughts and recollections. I hope my journey comes alive for you. I have been blessed and happy by the many opportunities and wonderful people who have touched my life.

The title of my story comes from Joyce Buekers, founder of The Harp Foundation. A few years ago, Joyce asked me to tell the story of how the harp became such an important part of my life. Joyce was playing the harp softly while I was speaking, and Pat Poulsen was recording it. Later he produced the DVD with the cover title *"Marie's Journey of Love.*

Many years ago, my sister Margo and her husband George came to visit me at Stanford, CA. On my desk was a card with words from George Bernard Shaw. Margo copied it and, what a surprise! Yes, a Christmas gift arrived from Margo and George. She wrote the words on a linen cloth, and then embroidered, decorated, and framed it. It is on the wall in our home. It has inspired me for all these years, and I treasure it! I share it with all of you, my dear readers.

> *Life is no "brief candle" to me. It is a sort of splendid torch which I have got hold of for the moment; and I want to make it burn as brightly as possible before handing it on to future generations.*
>
> George Bernard Shaw

Forward - *Joyce and Mike Buekers*

A mark of intelligence is being able to surround yourself with people who empower you and know more about your treasured values than you. Our values have always been centered on unconditional LOVE, UNITY and COMPASSION.

The seed for this book, **Marie's Journey of Love**, encompasses all of these values as well as friendships, families and a foundation. It continues to grow and blossom with Marie's guidance as an Advisory Board Member to The Harp Foundation...That first meeting with Marie and Del Grandstaff planted a seed that has continued to grow for us as a couple since the spring of 2003.

Her life story has been a joy for us at so many levels—truly LOVE summarizes it all. Chapters 1-3--*The Journey Begins, A Decision to be Made* and *Memories of her Teen Years* have been inspiring to our family. Marie's 18 brothers and sisters growing up on a farm with such spiritual values, work ethics and educational focus is revealed with LOVE in these chapters.

Chapters 4-10, *A New Chapter in My Life, A New Dream to Go OverSeas, On to College, Bound to Indonesia, Farewell to Willy, Turning Fear into Faith* and *Hope and Cruising into New Adventures* shows UNITY of Spirit. It is inspiring to our family as we travel and see the global visions that Marie has had her entire life.

Chapters 11-16, *The Road to Del, Our Magical New Life Together; Love of Music, Twist of Fate, Two Close Calls!* And *Celebration from*

Birth to Rebirth tells us her COMPASSION. How to listen to those gifts that come into our lives every day.

One of The Harp Foundation's board members wanted to give the ***gift*** of harp music for Marie's dear husband, Del Grandstaff, who had been placed in a hospice memory care unit where our therapeutic harp program had been playing for many years. Del was restless and in a great deal of pain and Joyce met the couple on a patio where the sun was shining. The arrival of the harp changed the entire atmosphere for the couple. Del's breath immediately started slowing; a smile was on his face as he fell in love with the majesty and beauty of the harp. According to Marie, he was able to relax from the pain for the first time in months. Marie subsequently called the foundation office and requested regular therapeutic harp sessions. One of our harpists joined them biweekly and as Del's passing came near, Marie requested *"Jesu Joy of Man's Desiring"* which was played during his transition. Through this COMPASSION and gift Del passed away calmly and peacefully and harps were present at his Celebration of Life Services.

This chapter in Marie's life planted a seed in our souls that soon began to blossom. With a gentle nudging from dreams of Del, at the age of 75, this seed began with the initial purchase of her very own harp. After her first strum on the resonant strings and their reverberation, she became a kindred spirit.

After two years of playing, nurturing her soul and committing her mind, heart and fingers to the harp, she had the opportunity to purchase a therapeutic harp for the hospital play for patients. Later, to her surprise, she found out that she actually had her own heart issues. She was due to share her story at a major fund-raiser for The Harp Foundation and did not arrive! We got the call that she had a major stroke. We arrived at her bedside with red roses and a small red harp to play for her.

Upon arrival at the hospital, we were told she had moved to a new wing of the hospital. So, while she was intentionally blessing others, her emotional, physical and spiritual heart was also being ministered to. Every day while at the hospital, harpists arrived from all over the Valley. Knowing how much Marie loved the harp, her cardiologist, Dr. Pozun, prescribed for her to play daily as part of her healing plan.

"Marie's Journey of Love" shows that LOVE, UNITY and COMPASSION can serve many others. Her involvement with The Angel Song program has not only benefited many patients and children at the hospital, but it has allowed a partnership to be developed with the Sun Health Foundation, Banner Del Webb Hospital and members of the Sun Cities communities. This has strengthened the visibility and prominence of The Harp Foundation in the west valley. We now can continues to expand and enhance our programs to children and adults who are facing critical medical issues.

Marie connects with many causes at the heart level--- for spiritual support, for her personal therapeutic needs as a harpist and now with patients and those of you who have the privilege of reading this wonderful journey. How about writing your own and sharing it with us as well and we all continue on our own journeys!

Marie's Journey of Love

Forward - *Susan Seats*

I was fortunate to have met Marie several years ago. I was struck by her gracious presence and the eloquence of her spoken words. She has a generous heart, and great affection for her family and friends. Her involvement in the community, church, Grail, and The Harp Foundation has helped many in need. I felt I was in the presence of an angelic spirit. I am sure Marie is very special to many of us who have had the privilege of knowing her.

The first time I visited Marie was a memorable experience. The first thing you notice when you enter her home is her beautiful grand piano and majestic golden harp. I was invited to sit down as she played each with great passion and joy. I was struck by the nurturing and beautiful environment of her home. Her walls and dressers are adorned with pictures of family. Shelves house many photo scrapbooks of trips spanning thirty-five countries. Unique paintings and objects fill her cozy home with memories of a rich and full life. We enjoyed a delicious meal at a table outdoors, surrounded by her lush desert garden which borders a golf course. Marie showed me a collection of journals she began writing years ago. I encouraged her to leave these journals for her loved ones, and thus this book began.

Marie has a flair for writing, and has written for many publications. She helped in the writing, translation, and/or editing of three books: *Women at the Crossroads* (translated from Indonesian), *The Call of the Hibiscus,* and *A Man in Essence,* folk tales from Irian Jaya, an island in Indonesia.

It was my privilege to assist Marie in sharing her *Journey of Love*. After hearing many of her stories, I realized it would take volumes to capture her life. I have taken her journal writings and done some editing with the help of friends. Marie's dear friend Lesa has assembled the pictures and written the poetry in the book. I hope you enjoy Marie's journey as much as I have.

Susan Seats

Forward – *Lesa-Caldarella-Wong*

I first heard about Marie from a Symphony of the West Valley board member, who told me that she and her husband Del had hosted an event in their home earlier that year, and that they were avid music lovers.

I vividly remember the first time I walked into their home. You could sense the joy and feel the vibration of memories in that sacred place. Marie gave me a tour and recounted the history attached to every decorative item. It was like a museum of charm and adventure; there was special sentiment behind every photo, book, pillow, plate, and painting.

She had the most pure and delightful outlook on her life's journey, and a profound gratitude stemming from her love for "her Del." She was clearly thankful for their life together and the blessing of meeting him in their golden years. She spoke of him with adoration and affection. Theirs was a predestined love story, rich and abundant.

She and I had tea and talked for many hours, and found that our lives had a number of parallels. We both came from large loving families; we both love our Catholic faith and traditions; we love music and food. And each of us had taken a path that led us to ministry and gave us the opportunity to travel far away to worlds beyond the sanctuary of our families—she went to Indonesia and I went to Africa. We talked about how we were forever transformed and shaped by the broadening of our worldview, of how seeing the simplicity of life, deep-seated spirituality, and even the poverty enriched our lives.

Although Marie is only two years younger than my own mother, our ages did not matter. I felt, during that first five-hour tea time, that I had gained a dear friend. Each of us remarked that we felt there was a special purpose in our meeting.

It is with gratitude that I count Marie as a friend and sister of the soul, someone I will always treasure and hold close to my heart. Marie's life journey is inspiring and a testament to her joy, her love of people, and her passion to serve. Her path is gracefully and frequently intertwined with music and her profound spirituality. I am blessed to know her, her story, her life, and this book.

Chapter 1

The Journey Begins

It was a beautiful early morning in Kansas, May 19, 1929. I chose that day to say hello to the world and become the fifth child of a wonderful family. My father, grandmother, and family doctor announced to mother, "It's a healthy baby girl!" Wow! Three brothers and a big sister were awaiting me. How lucky can one be? All of us Mohr children

The Mohr Family; John, Clarence, Catherine, Nicholas, Joseph, Michael, Marie, Josephine, William, Peter, Ann, Bartel, "Mother," Theresa, "Father," Gregory, Al, Anthony, and Francis

were delivered at home by our family doctor. Grandma was thrilled because she would be my godmother. She became an important person in my early years, and I grew to love her very much.

As the years passed, we welcomed four more sisters and nine more brothers into our family, the proud eighteen children of Peter and Anna Mohr. Memories of my childhood are filled with exciting family times. We liked to keep active by playing ball and croquet in our yard, and by going fishing in our creek and ponds. We had a lot of fun rowing the boat down the creek, from the dam all the way to the cabin. Catfish, carp, ducks, geese, quail, pheasants, and wild turkeys liked to roam our pasture. Years later, deer would also graze there.

My sister Jose and I often played house in my childhood. Saturday was mom's baking day, and she and Catherine, my older sister, made pies, cakes, cinnamon rolls and, of course, delicious homemade bread. When we were too small to help bake, we would bring our little cake and pie dishes, and Mom would give us some of the real thing to serve on our cute little table and chairs. We pretended we were grown-up ladies having tea parties. These are memories that still touch my heart today.

In addition to the many joyful hours of play and adventures, we learned at an early age the value of good hard work. Vegetable gardens and fruit orchards all required planting, weeding, harvesting, and then preserving huge amounts of food for the cold winter months. Of course, being on a farm, there were also animals to care for. Chickens, cattle, and pigs provided us with fresh eggs and meat throughout the year.

The time soon arrived to prepare for the adventure of starting school! On the first day, registration made me feel like I was entering a foreign world. I was used to speaking German at home. Grandma accompanied me and told the teacher my name was "Mary Anne Mohr."

Joseph's ordination, prior to Willie's passing and the last time the entire family was assembled together

Puzzled, I looked at her and said, "my name is Marie." To this day, the official records bear the name "Mary Anne Mohr." I thoroughly enjoyed learning and academic challenges. The teachers were nuns, and they were caring and wonderful, especially during my first years. My brothers, sisters, and I were blessed with intelligence and performed well in school. All of us are bilingual, and some of us are multilingual.

Our transportation was quite unique. My oldest brothers would harness dear Daisy to the buggy, five or six of us would climb up into the carriage, and off we'd go. It was five miles from home to school. It was pretty cold in the winter, but the memories of those travels are mostly very pleasant. My brother Nick would read to us from the much-loved Father Finn storybooks. Starting in the fourth grade, my father drove us to school in our car.

The Mohr household was very active. We experienced the usual sibling battles, and as my brother John said, "There was never a dull moment at our home." Meals were enjoyed at our large dining room table. My parents instilled in us a great love for music. Dad bought an accordion, and later a piano. Love songs, German folk songs, and hymns were all part of our song fests. What a thrill it was when dad came home with an Edison record player with a gold-tipped needle. It still plays today.

Between the record player and the radio, we learned to appreciate all kinds of music, including classical. Most of the Mohr children sang, whether in the church choir, driving in the car, working in the garden, or while doing chores at home. My childhood recollections are happy ones. I am thankful for the music, good cooking, baking, and, most of all, the love shared with my parents and dear sisters and brothers. I was also lucky to be surrounded with the caring love of extended family—grandparents, and a number of aunts, uncles, and cousins. In fact, I believe the experiences of my growing-up years have significantly contributed to the kind of person I am today, eighty years later.

Our after-school snack was a delicious piece of mom's freshly baked bread with butter and jelly. After the snack, the boys milked the cows, and we girls picked up the eggs from the henhouse and then help mom make dinner. After that, we studied and did homework. When we were through, we usually ended the evening with singing and prayers.

World War II caused much anguish in our family. In 1890, Grandpa had left his native country to live in America. When the United States went to war against Germany, they were fighting against his homeland. These were traumatic years for all Germans who had come to live in America, as their children were fighting against family relatives in Europe. Speaking German was forbidden at school and in public places. Internment camps were set up for targeted Germans, and two of my cousins, unfortunately, were sent to them. I was young and did not understand all that was going on.

It was a tradition that we stopped at our grandparents' on our way home from school, especially to show our report cards. Once I had a low mark in "conduct," Grandpa, with a stern look, sat me on his lap and asked what this was about. I told him the teacher caught me speaking German. Grandpa asked, "Did this happen during class?" "No," I replied, "it was during recess when I talked with my sister Josephine." I'll never forget his answer! "Oh, that poor teacher doesn't know that to speak two languages is better than knowing just one, and to speak three languages is even better." Perhaps that motivated me to learn more languages. This often comes to mind as I enjoy the gift of communication with many people around the world in their native tongue, and later as an interpreter for the State Department.

At school, our pastor could be very strict, yet I was quite fond of him. He taught religion, and when he came to the chapter on the seven sacraments, he said, "I will wait until Marie has a new brother or sister before teaching about the sacrament of Baptism." The long-awaited day arrived when my sister was born in February. Can you imagine my pride and joy when I was chosen to be her godmother? My first godchild, my sweet baby sister Theresa! All my classmates were invited to attend the baptism.

One day in religion class, Monsignor was talking to us about the Trinity, and I was puzzled. I said, "In the Trinity, I can understand the Father and the Son, but the Holy Ghost (term used in the 50's) is not clear." His answer still supersedes any explanation given by hundreds

Marie at her eight grade graduation from Saint Marks, 1942

of preachers or religious teachers. He said," Marie, just think of it as the love that exists between the Father and the Son." Amen! So be it!

I recall that when graduation day was quickly approaching, I was already thinking about my future and asked Monsignor what vocation he thought I was best suited for. He looked at me kindly, took my hand,

and replied, "Marie, I can see you as a mother superior in a convent. But I can also see you as a wonderful mother of a large family, just like your own mother. In other words, search your heart and let your spirit speak within you. You are the one who has to decide."

Marie's Journey of Love

Chapter 2

A Decision to be Made

Graduation day arrived. Because of my good grades, I was awarded a scholarship to an all-girl Catholic high school in Wichita, Kansas. My parents talked it over. "Marie," they said, "if you want to become a teacher, nun, or nurse, we will let you take advantage of this opportunity." My decision was clear; I longed to continue my education, since I'd always enjoyed school. However, the only path I wanted was to study music. That was not to be. Grandma Mohr entered the conversation and reminded us that a cousin in Germany had studied voice and sang with an opera company but, sadly, she had stopped going to church. From her perspective, it was a dangerous career to pursue. Well, that took care of that decision. I felt disappointed and decided that my limited school options did not fit my dreams. Instead, I stayed home and helped my parents and family. Some of my brothers were away at a boarding school in Oklahoma, and our parents needed help and support from all of us. How they managed such a large family with so much love and caring still remains a mystery to me.

Seven of my brothers were drafted into the military. Five were sent to Germany, another went to Korea, and the oldest went to the

South Pacific. Imagine the heartache of parents seeing their young sons off to war. Will they come home safely? What hardships and difficulties will they face in the prime of their lives? No doubt many a parent has suffered sleepless nights under these conditions. Asking God to protect and safeguard them became part of our daily prayers as a family. There was joy and excitement for every letter that was received from them, assuring us of their safety and well-being.

On our farm, there was a big lawn in the front where we often played ball and croquet with our parents. The farm presented us with some unusually hard work, which we girls learned to do since most of our brothers had been sent off to the military. My sister Jose, a year younger than me, and I learned the fine art of shucking corn. Someone would put us in the wagon, which was hitched up to the horses, and send us into the cornfield to bring home a harvest of ripe ears. This we did successfully a number of times, although we had a near-disastrous experience.

On the ride home from the field, the horses spooked and tore loose into what is called "a runaway team." We were in the wagon, pulling the reins and yelling stop, but it did not make a bit of difference. They just kept running faster. Crossing at the corner, a speeding car raced right in front of us. Dear God, what a close call! We were badly shaken up. Since I am here years later to tell the story, you know the outcome. My brother later teased me saying, "Marie, you made the horse go there so you could visit Ralph." Ralph was a boy from my school whose house was nearby.

My sisters and I also helped other families when they had a new baby. We had to take over the care of the household. Cooking, cleaning, and taking care of their other children were often our responsibility.

Farm families in those days were often very large. The most important task was giving the newborn a daily bath and tending to the needs of the mother, who would often rest in bed for the first week. Most of these deliveries were home births with a doctor, not a midwife. While doing family service, I encountered my first bald baby. All of mom and dad's babies were so adorable, sporting full heads of hair. When I came home that night, my parents wanted to know who the new baby looked like. I said, "Well the baby is bald and not very pretty." Dad immediately corrected me. "All babies are beautiful, innocent and sweet." Some of these families were pleasant and really appreciated our help; however, some of the families were pretty tough and gave us real challenges. It helped me love and appreciate my parents and our loving home environment even more.

Marie's Journey of Love

Chapter 3

Memories of my Teen Years

An important family tradition began during my early teen years. Dad, mom, and our cousin, Dr. Lies, planned the first of what would become our annual Fourth of July picnics. Our farm, with its creeks and ponds, made it an ideal setting. Extended family and some of our priests joined in the fun. Everyone brought their favorite dishes. There were usually more than 100 people who attended the now-yearly occasion. A keg of beer and wide variety of drinks for the kids were on hand. There were plenty of games and sports, like cards and baseball. It was an excellent way to get to know each other and to talk about our lives. Even after mom and dad passed on, we continued our picnics in their honor until 2006. As time unfolded we became the adults, aunts and uncles to many nieces and nephews. We allowed them to bring a friend, and their friends became part of our family as well. In the afternoon, I would get out my accordion and we'd sing together. Many drove a long way, and those who lingered ended up around the piano for another sing-along. This was truly a major event, and one we all looked forward to. Del, my husband, felt that this was one of the highlights of our years together.

Marie's Journey of Love

Just as my deep love for music never faltered, I also enjoyed dancing. The youth groups from all the country parishes gathered in Colwich for a weekly dance. Sometimes, due to anticipation, I was ready to leave for the dance without eating dinner. Mom would say, "Marie, you eat first and then you can go." The jitterbug was a lot of fun with all the twirling and quick steps, especially with a good partner. My older brother Mike was a very good dancer.

The events sponsored by the church's youth club were also a lot of fun. We took several hayrides to our family's creek and picnic area. Bales of hay were used as seats on the trailers, which were pulled by a tractor. Loud and enthusiastic singing filled the air as we traveled the five-mile stretch from the church to our home. Drinks and food were unpacked, and games were played on the grassy areas, to everyone's delight. The ride home in the moonlight was special and could be romantic, especially if you cuddled up close to one of the boys who made your heart flutter.

I dated a number of young men during those years. An older boy named Bert, whom I thought was interested in my older sister, asked me for a date. He sang tenor in our choir. I always thought he was handsome, but it was his younger brother who made my heart skip a beat whenever he came near. Nevertheless, I accepted Bert's offer and we went to the big city of Wichita to see Harry Blackstone, the magician. I was so impressed and, to this day, still enjoy magic shows. Sometime after that memorable evening, young men started coming home from the army, and more of them invited me to go out with them.

I truly enjoyed those dates, but not all of my social activities had parental blessings. One fellow, who was a year ahead of me in grammar school, asked me to be his date for the big football banquet. Even though

I was not in high school, he still invited me. What a disappointment when mom and dad said I could not go. There was some belief about not dancing on Saturday night back in those days. Yes, as Christian Catholics, there were some strict rules we had to live by. My parents became more open-minded and less conservative over the years. They were able to provide for all of us, guide us, and give us an example of deeply Christian parents totally committed to their children, church, and community. The values they instilled in me have given me the courage and strength to endure and survive a number of serious challenges. Their generosity, love, and kindness were a gift to all of us, and to the many whose lives they touched. My heart is forever grateful to both of them.

I loved helping my little brothers and sisters get ready to go out. Once, when mom and I were walking to church with the little ones—Margo, Greg and Theresa—I asked mom, "Don't you wish they would always stay this age? Look how happy and cute they are." Her reply, with that special smile on her face, was "They are also very nice when they are grown-up." What a sweet compliment that was for me.

I enjoyed sewing clothes for my two younger sisters. One day, while making similar outfits for Margo and Theresa, little brother Greg came up to me. He was so small that his face could barely be seen above the sewing machine "Who is that for?" he asked. "For your two sisters," I replied. "Why do you always sew something for them and not for me?" I remedied that right there and then. I showed him some fabrics, and he chose a small red-checkered piece. Immediately I cut out a little shirt for him. He was so happy. Of course, we did sew lots of shorts and shirts for the little boys, but his new one was special.

When Margo was only a few months old, she became very sick. Mom had been up with her all night. In the early morning she called the doctor. He said, "Take her to the hospital immediately and I will meet you there." Mom asked me to dress the baby while she and dad got themselves ready. After they left, I returned to the bedroom, threw myself on the bed and started to sob. The older children came in and said, "Stop crying, she will be all right." "No, she was already getting stiff. She was almost dead." We soon learned that her little back was very stiff because of spinal meningitis. I loved that baby as if she were my own. Imagine the prayers that stormed the heavens. Margo survived, and what a gift she has been to our family and the many others who have been touched by the beauty of her life and her caring and generous spirit.

I have often said, "Thank God mom and dad welcomed so many precious souls into our family. Each one has brought a unique and special gift to share with the others." It is amazing how different we each are as individuals, yet we are one family sharing a bond of love and friendship. The ups and downs have been there, but the joys and love far outweigh all the sorrow and sadness.

My dear parents inspired us all with their profound and deep faith in God. As Catholic Christians, we went to church every Sunday, prayed before and after meals, and said the family rosary in May and October. Their daily examples of care, discipline, love, and generosity taught us so much. They encouraged us to follow our hearts and live our lives with faith and love.

All their eighteen children chose numerous vocations or professions—farmers, nurses, a medical doctor, construction and bus company workers, a priest, a nun, three US Government employees, three or four teachers, and family service. Since we are all bilingual, it's no surprise!

Two brothers taught German and Spanish. I taught the national Indonesian language for ten years at Stanford University, plus I was an interpreter for the US Department of State and a translator in Java and Bali, Indonesia.

What a story. Ten of us lived and worked overseas—Libya, Korea, Singapore, Iran, Scotland, France, Germany, Southeast and Indonesia.

Yes, quite a record! All the family was born in the heartland of Kansas and grew up on a beautiful family farm. Our parents taught us to think and appreciate global world views and concerns. My sisters and brothers-in-law are also valued and loved. They are great!

What blessing to have a mother and a father who nurtured and loved us so much, and still do.

One year was decreed a holy year by the pope, and my cousin and his wife decided to go to Rome during the celebrations to participate in a month of special prayers and services. They asked my parents if I could come to their house and take over the responsibility of caring for their four children while they were gone. Mom and Dad hesitated and asked if the children could stay at our house so I could care for them there. "No," they said, "that would not be possible, since two of the children go to school and two stay at home." Some challenging moments did occur during that month, but I dearly loved the children. Upon my cousin's return to the United States, we were given a generous payment for all the work and concern. Rosie, the baby, had forgotten who her mother was, and clung to me when her mother tried to take her. The couple said, "Now, Marie, be sure to use this money for something special just for you."

Marie's Journey of Love

Springtime in my childhood home, Wichita, Kansas

Sheep grazing on the family farm

Annual July 4th Mohr Family Reunion Celebration

Chapter 4

A New Chapter in My Life

A friend of mine had mentioned that she wanted to go to Chicago in the fall for a college entrance interview. She also wanted to take a class about women in the modern world in Ohio. I was glad I had earned some extra money which allowed me to go as well. Four of us decided to make the trip together. We had become good friends during the dances at Colwich. My father helped book our train rides and a hotel in the big city of Chicago. We had a beautiful view overlooking the lake, and a really good time. Can you picture four young girls from Kansas exploring the big city? We signed up for the course at Grailville, and from there we headed to Loveland, Ohio.

Those days with the International Grail women marked the beginning of a new chapter in my life. Grailville is a community of women from many countries, cultures, and very different backgrounds. Although the Grail organization is grounded in the Christian faith, women from diverse religious backgrounds have also been welcomed. In my own life, I probably would have taken a totally different direction without this encounter of women from many parts of the world.

A predictable future for me would have been a return to Kansas, marriage with some fine young man, and the raising of a family in the tradition of my parents.

Well, that was not to be. Deep in my soul I knew I must return and start a new life with the Grail women, whose members shared a desire to find meaningful ways of contributing to the transformation of our world into a place of love, unity, and justice, where every child can bloom and flourish. Where would this new path lead me? I did not know, but I knew I must return to answer a profound call to explore the next part of my life's journey.

> *Two roads diverged in a wood, and I-*
> *I took the one less traveled by,*
> *And that has made all the difference.*
>   *Robert Frost*

I returned home filled with new inspiration. In the fall, the Grail offered a new training for the lay apostolate. I begged my parents to let me go. Somehow my explanation did not convince them that this was a great choice. Finally, in January, my Dad took me aside and we had a good talk. "We see that you will not be happy until you take this opportunity to go back to Ohio." "Yes, Dad, you are right." My dear dad began preparations for the trip to Ohio, and soon off I went. It was difficult to say good-bye to my beloved sisters, brothers, and parents, but in my heart I knew this had to be the next step in my life.

Marie Mohr

Mom packed a delicious lunch for the train, and my dear father took me to the station after huge good-byes. He also put some extra cash in my pocket and said, "Now be sure and go to the dining car and have at least one warm meal." This was a long journey. Once the train pulled out of the station, my tears flowed for a long time. Oh, how I missed them already, goodness!

Someone from the Grail was at the Loveland, Ohio train station to meet me. Grailville was located on a large farm. There was a gracious three-story house surrounded by many other farm buildings, including a chicken house, granaries, and some guilds. I was taken to a shed above a large garage. It was originally for horses, but now our sleeping quarters were in the former stalls. I was given the top of a bunk bed. I always felt a bit apprehensive hoisting myself up to the top at night. The pangs of

Marie's Journey of Love

homesickness were most severe at night when I didn't fall asleep right away. The sound of the train whistle in the night from the small town of Loveland made me want to climb out of bed, run to the train, and hope it would take me back to my warm, loving family.

Another young woman arrived from New York the same day I did. Her name was Eva Fleischner, a lovely person, who has remained a close friend ever since, even though our paths eventually took different directions. At Grailville, we were both in the choir ,and this created a deep bond between us. The music rehearsals were the best part, along with the many great lectures we had during the first year, which included speakers like Maria Von Trapp of *The Sound of Music*; Don Vincent Martin, a missionary in China; Monsignor Ligutti; Dom Vitry from France; and too many more to mention.

Marie, Dr. Janet Kalven, and Dr. Lydwin Von Kersbergen, President Women's International Grail Movement

Dr. Lydwin Von Kersbergen and her staff instilled in us a great desire to use our womanly qualities of compassion and understanding to help bring unity and peace to the entire world. These first few years were very vigorous and with few creature comforts. We had outdoor johns, or "lilies," as we called them, and basic but healthy foods from our garden.

After learning that I was a fairly good seamstress, I was placed in the sewing guild. A wonderful woman named Lydia was in charge. She was referred to as our "housemother." That never worked for me since I felt so deeply proud of my own mother and felt no need for another, and so to me she was just "Lydia from Holland." We had a great time. I sewed the costumes for our folk dance group. I was also a member and loved dancing on Sunday nights. I also helped sew vestments which were decorated by the beautiful woven trims made on the looms in the sewing guild.

Grailville provided me with many opportunities to continue the broad world perspective that was instilled in me by my parents. The lectures given by our own residence staff were informative, educational, and inspirational. Yes, it was difficult work, especially with our rustic living conditions, but it helped us build character and develop the courage to face the challenges of the modern world. Major emphasis was placed on the role that women were to play in helping to achieve a world of peace and unity.

After several years of preparation, I was transferred to the new international student center in New York City. What a contrast to the life I had known having lived mainly in the country! St Patrick's Cathedral was our parish, and near enough for a nice daily walk to mass. We collaborated with the chaplain at Columbia University, where we met with students from all around the world. This was my cup of tea—international and ecumenical! It all seemed so good and important in our striving for world peace.

In one of my first letters home, I wrote that I deeply missed the open spaces like those back home. Imagine, I wrote, in order to see the sky you have to go down the street and look up. No awe-inspiring sunsets or sunrises. The beauty of nature was hidden by the tall skyscrapers. I endured some powerful bouts of homesickness during these first few months, but I soon became enamored with the many things a big city has to offer. I was within walking distance of the Metropolitan Opera House and lectures at the university. We later moved to larger quarters at Riverside Drive, where we had a magnificent view of the Hudson River. What a welcome change!

THE GRAIL

Called by our spiritual values, The Grail envisions a world of peace, justice and renewal of the earth, brought about by women working together as catalysts for change.

Who we are

We are an international women's movement empowering women to work for world transformation. We are committed to spiritual search, social transformation, ecological sustainability, and the release of women's creative energy throughout the world.

Our Goals

Building bridges among diverse faith traditions and spiritual paths

Advancing peace, justice and a world free from military dominance

Fostering international exchange and solidarity

Challenging economic systems that put at risk the most vulnerable, especially women and children

Creating communities for a sustainable future

Celebrating the arts as a means for personal and societal transformation

---

THE GRAIL IS WORKING IN 17 COUNTRIES WORLDWIDE!

We have centers or groups in:
Australia, Brazil, Canada, Germany, Italy, Kenya, Mexico, Mozambique, Netherlands, Papua New Guinea, Philippines, Portugal, South Africa, Sweden, Tanzania, Uganda, and the USA.

The International Grail has its activities organized into several networks/groups. Through these networks Grail women work together to fulfill the mission and vision of The Grail.

Networks:
The Grail is an NGO in consultative status with ECOSOC at the United Nations
Global Justice/Overcoming Poverty
Human Trafficking
Women of the Americas
Earth, Ecology & Bio-Diversity

OUR U.S. CENTERS:

THE GRAIL
932 O'Bannonville Road
Loveland, OH 45140
Phone: (513) 683-5750
Email: office@grail-us.org
www.grail-us.org

GRAILVILLE
Phone: (513) 683-2340
Email: grailville@fuse.net
www.grailville.org

CORNWALL ON HUDSON
Phone: (845) 534-2031
Email: grailconh@igc.org
www.thegrailatcornwall.org

THE BRONX
Phone: (718) 665-0271
Email: bronxgrail@juno.com

Marie's Journey of Love

Chapter 5

A New Dream: To Go Overseas

A few years later, we opened an Institute for Overseas Service in Brooklyn. Joining the staff here proved to be quite a rewarding challenge. After a year or so, I made it clear that I wanted to spend some time overseas as a lay missionary with the Grail. Discussions began with our international and national leaders, Rachel and Lydwine. They asked me to consider a post in Indonesia. The woman from Holland who was there now was planning to return to the Netherlands. They also said that visas were more readily obtained if one had a college degree. What a dilemma. Remember, I had forfeited my high school scholarship to stay home and help my family.

Janet Kalven, our staff member, was very knowledgeable about all academic matters. She talked to me about the equivalency exam for those waiting to complete a high school diploma, and proceeded to get in touch with the gentleman in charge of this program in our area. He explained the procedure and time frame. Exams were to be held the following week; the next ones would not be held for several months. I felt that I needed time to study and prepare. He tried to allay my fears by saying, "Just by speaking with you, my suggestion is that you sign up for next week. If you don't pass, you can try again." He added that at least fifty percent of students didn't pass on the first try. He said, "If you don't pass, at least you will have a good idea of what to expect the second time." The classes were held at a Brooklyn high school at night. It took a great deal of courage, or should I say guts, to take the exam. There was a large crowd of all ages and types—policemen, firemen, and others—all hoping to complete the high school requirements. The whole idea was nerve-wracking, but this was necessary to fulfill my dream of going overseas to serve and to work for peace on a global scale.

The reading test went well. When I came back to the center, my dear friend Catherine was waiting with a selection of coffee, tea, or hot chocolate. "How did it go?" she asked. Well, I felt quite confident that it had gone well. I felt relieved. The next night was spelling; still no problem. Then composition, and another great sigh of relief, which was short-lived—the next exam was algebra. I had never been exposed to algebra in grammar school, and felt overwhelmed. Catherine did her best to cheer me up, but I knew that part of the test was a total blackout. After quite some time, the results came, "You have passed the exam, and here is your diploma"! No mention of the scores or of grade given, just compliments at having achieved the first victory of my educational goals.

Life continued at the Overseas Institute, and I was given numerous responsibilities. Our prominent list of lecturers came from the prestigious Fordham University. My own world view continued to become stronger and more informed. I was introduced to the remarkable writings of Father Teilhard de Chardin. This great man, in addition to my own parents and a few other individuals, played a major role in deepening my own spiritual life, world perspectives, and human destiny. My heart is forever grateful. His books, *Divine Milieu* and *Phenomenon of Man*, plus other writings, continue to inspire me and strengthen my hope that the human family will wake up and realize the power they have to achieve a new level of consciousness.

Marie's Journey of Love

Chapter 6

On to College!

In order to realize my dream of helping people overseas, specifically Indonesia, I had to consider the next step—a college degree. A friend helped arrange an appointment at Pratt Institute, a fine school and within walking distance of our Grail center. My meeting was with Dr. Dean Rabineau a tall, handsome man who was gentle and easy to talk with. After explaining my situation, he replied, "Let me think about this and discuss it with the staff. We will be in touch."

After some time, I was called back to the office of Dean Rabineau. His smiling face was most reassuring. "We have come to a decision. You will be the first student admitted with your credentials. The equivalency diploma results showed that you scored in the top ten percent of the nation's high school graduates, so we are willing to take you on probation in the fall. If you do well, then, of course, you can continue."

It was summer, so hooray! I had a chance to prepare. Janet prepared some transfer credits for me from the informal study of Grailville, which had an affiliation with the Catholic University in Washington, DC.

Imagine my mixed feelings as the opening day of school approached. What would it be like, sitting in a classroom of freshmen? Obviously, they would all be younger than I was. But all my fears and trepidation soon disappeared as I buried myself in the study requirements. What a joy to find that, at the end of the first semester, I had made the honor roll. This continued, and in two years I graduated with honors. This included several summer courses taken at New York University's downtown campus. I became an expert at riding the underground subways. They are an effective and rapid means of transit, but to this day I dislike riding underground anywhere in the world. Ask my friends; they will tell you I'd rather spend extra time on the city bus to get to my destination.

During that time I continued living at the Grail center. I worked as a bookkeeper. I also helped to lead the choir. Before long, Baidy and I began to prepare for our transfer to Indonesia. I was assigned to serve with several of our members who were already working on the island of Java. Bishop Carroll from Wichita, Kansas, was pleased to hear that a former member of his diocese would be going to Indonesia as a lay missionary person. He was a dear friend of our family, and used to call our mother "mom." Local newspapers there carried stories about my new adventure, much to the delight of my family.

(See addendum for these newspaper articles.)

Chapter 7

Bound For Indonesia

Lydwine and Rachael did a wonderful job of making the arrangements for my trip to Southeast Asia. Plans included a stop at the Amsterdam Grail International Headquarters to visit Monsignor Fittkau, a dear family friend in Germany, and a side trip to Mayen, where I would meet my cousin Klotilde Mohr and her family. Next, a short but exciting visit in Egypt to meet with our team stationed there. It gave me the opportunity to see my dear classmate from New York, Nefissa Gohar. What a thrill to see the pyramids, the magnificent Sphinx, and many other ancient and memorable sites. I was in awe of all these wonders. A special thrill was a visit to the church assumed to be the one Joseph, Mary and Jesus fled to when escaping from King Herod. What an amazing variety of experiences I had!

Mixed feelings raced through my whole being as they announced it was time to fasten our seat belts—we would soon be landing in Jakarta. I am sure Baidy, our Philippine Grail member, was also excited, but in a different way. After all, this would not be so completely new to her. The climate, flora, and fauna were similar to that in her country.

Francine and Benedict met us at the airport, where we received warm greetings and headed to a restaurant before embarking on our long journey to the city of Semarang in Central Java. No one had prepared me for my first bathroom encounter. To my dismay, it was simply a hole in the floor. "Oh goodness, there's no toilet paper!" Thank God I had Kleenex. I came back to the table somewhat embarrassed and mentioned that there wasn't any toilet paper. "Didn't you see the bottles of water on the floor? That is what you use to clean your bottom," replied Francine. Much later, I would share this story with my students at Stanford University, where I taught the Indonesian language and cross-cultural training classes for ten years.

I thought of a prayer that would capture my life's work: **let my life be a gift, let me share all I can give to others, and especially let my heart be filled with love. Amen.**

This was the beginning of an adventure where almost everything was new to me—the culture, people, language, food, sights, sounds, and even smells. Although it was an adjustment, the warm and friendly disposition of the people made a lasting good impression during my impressionable first days. What a contrast we had traveling from the noisy crowded streets of Jakarta to the quiet beauty of the countryside. I was captivated and filled with a sense of wonder. The mountains in Java are truly majestic. The magnificent terraced rice fields seemed to rise up to the heavens. There were many palm trees swaying in the gentle breeze. Brightly colored bougainvilleas cascaded along the fences. It was nature in her full glory! Bordering the path were lovely red poinsettias, unique with their full blossoms in large trees. Rice fields and tea plantations were clustered on the hillside. It was a true sensory delight!

What an interesting experience to see the different types of transportation on the roads. Careful, here comes an ox pulling a cart!

Wow, so many bicycles and motor scooters, some with four or five family members on one bike! *Betjak*, three-wheeled vehicles, were everywhere along the road, and usually carried two people riding with a driver behind. Many of the Indonesian people are quite small in stature, and sometimes four or five family members would squeeze a little betjack. There were also many trucks and cars, and a collision could have quite serious consequences. Benedict and Francine drove a funny little French car called a Citroen. What a bumpy ride, sitting on a stretched-canvas seat. But I had no complaints, just a feeling of excitement and curiosity in my heart. I wondered what kind of adventures were waiting for us in the days ahead. We drove for miles and miles from Jakarta, passing through the charming town of Bogor. Up and up we went through the winding mountain roads to the city of Bandung, and on to Semarang. This was to be our home for several months before we reached the final goal of our destiny, Surabaja in East Java, where Baidy and I would live and work.

My dear teacher was Pak Karnadi, and we spent months with him in Semarang learning to speak Indonesian. I was determined to speak this strange and difficult language as quickly as possible. Rumor had it that I was a good student. We stayed focused on our jobs and learning and absorbing all we could of the culture. We were introduced to the performance of the Wayang Kulit, and the enchanted and haunting music of the Gamelan orchestra. Later in Surabaja I studied this ancient music with a student group from Airlangga University. What an exciting class that was. We became so proficient that we were invited to play on the radio!

My first three years in Indonesia included more musical experiences. I had shipped my lovely large accordion from New York, and was thrilled that it had arrived in my trunk. I purchased the accordion just for this purpose, and had paid for it with money earned by reading Christmas stories on a New York radio station. I learned as many of the Indonesian folk songs as I could. Many years later, when teaching at Stanford, the folk songs that I learned would be a highlight of many of my Indonesian language classes

What a proud occasion it was when Grail President Dr. Magdalene Oberhoffer came from Europe to visit our program. We created an evening to welcome and entertain her. We included our Indonesian members, who danced the lovely candle dance accompanied by my accordion.

The mellow and intriguing strains of *gamelan* music had touched my soul profoundly. An all-night performance with friends in Bandung is forever etched in my memory. The beautiful gong, an instrument used in gamelan music, resides in my Arizona home because of my dear husband, Del. During one of our travels, he experienced the sound of the gong, and decided that we must bring it back with us. It adorned our living room in Nevada near Lake Tahoe, and now it delights me here in my Arizona living room. When I leave this earth, it will go to the owners of the Osage Monastery Benedictine retreat center chapel in Oklahoma. They will enjoy it as it calls them to prayer.

After a number of months, we said our good-byes and headed to the East Java city of Surabaja. A member of the International Grail left to return to her home country in the Netherlands, and soon another person, Helena Fong, was sent back to the United States. Goodness, all so quick! Several students from the university and several teachers at a school nearby lived with us in a charming house on Teratai Street. We were a team, but a lot of the responsibilities fell on my shoulders. The bishop of the Diocese was friendly and helpful, and I quickly learned how to take charge of the many financial situations. Baidy, my dear teammate from the Philippines, became a teacher at the home economics school. I started a choir for a nearby church, where our pastor was Father Mensvoort. After a year or so, I was quite proficient with the language and was hired as a teacher at Widya Mandala University. The religion survey course was put together by a Jesuit in Jogya, a fine Presbyterian pastor in central Java, and me. It was a great learning experience. President Sukarno was strict, and he required a passing grade in religion in order to complete one's course of study at the university.

I taught several levels of English classes there, and the university is still thriving.

The memories of my musical adventures in Indonesia are truly precious. Memories of medical events however, were not very pleasant. During the flu season, I shared medications from my handy medicine bag which Dr. Lies from Kansas had packed before I left the states. I shared the sulfa tablets with my friends who came down with the flu, and they all recovered. Not so for me. I felt awful, and soon red pimples covered my body. They itched like hell! I got in touch with some of the staff from the United States who were working at Airlangga University, and with whom we were good friends, especially Dr. Paul and his family. I called his house, and Dr. Paul told me to come over immediately and spend several days at his home. "But Paul," I said, "what I have is the measles, and your three children might get them." The reason he suggested I come to his house was because we lived in a place with an Indonesian-style bathroom—no shower or tub, just a deep vat of water. Paul immediately figured out I was suffering from an allergy to the sulfur tablets. My ankles and mouth were swollen, and I had no appetite. He arranged a bath with baking soda, and told me to just lie and relax in the cool water. It immediately gave me some relief. This allergic reaction kept me home from school and teaching. Several of the doctors from the university came to visit. The first food that I could eat was chocolate. I learned the hard way that whenever I needed an antibiotic in the future, it would not be sulfa!

A second time, I became very sick with an ear infection. Lancing the eardrum was terribly painful, and every bump the betjack hit on the road hurt it even more. Gracious, there were many bumps! Each jolt made me want to scream out loud, but I had to be polite and gracious. I was glad to finally get back home. The only food I wanted to eat were the soup packets sent from mom. God bless my family for those monthly care packages.

Arriving in Jakarta, Indonesia

Marie having a jeep ride in Sulawesi

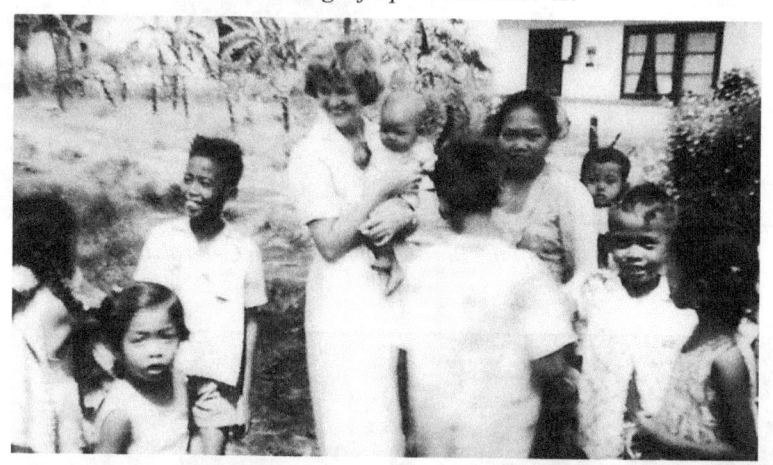

Marie at a Family Clinic in Java

Marie playing accordion at Grail Team Celebration

Marie's Journey of Love

On the steps of the Borobudur Temple in Central Java

Marie enjoying the typical Javanese transportation

Grail Team Library in Surabaya

The Grail Team enjoying the library

Marie teaching at Widya, Mandala University in Surabaya

Marie's Journey of Love

Solar eclipse ceremony in Java

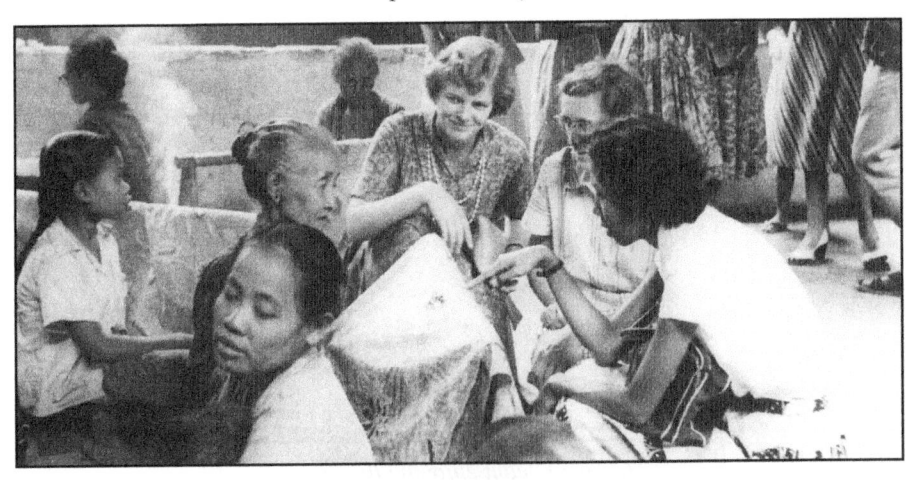

Marie visiting a batik factory

The Grail Team enjoying time together

Marie and friends celebrating

Religion and English class, Marie taught classes in both English and Indonesian

Marie's Journey of Love

Grail Team meeting

Marie wearing traditional silk Sulawesi dress to greet the President of Grail Germany, Dr. Oberhoffer

Marie and some of her Indonesian students give a musical performance for Col. Wakefield of London

Chapter 8

Farewell to Willy

Another memory of deep impact was when I left Indonesia to say a final good-bye to my dear brother William—Willy, as we called him. I learned that he was dying. He had been stationed in Korea for some years, and shortly after he came back they discovered he had cancer. Our family doctor said he may not be around long, so if I had a chance, I should come home. It was 1963 when I received special permission to make the trip.

It was a tender reunion, and we embraced for a long time. At that time, my brother was feeling a little better. He was home and could engage in some of his favorite activities, like fishing and gardening. One Sunday, Willie, my sister Jose, and I took my aunt back to her work as an assistant to a priest. Hoping to get some comfort, we all talked to Father Tockert about Willy's situation. He proceeded to preach about life, death, and the afterlife. He never asked my brother if he had any questions or concerns pertaining to his situation.

A couple of days later, I had a heart to heart talk with Willie while we were walking in the garden. "I noticed you were very quiet when Father Tockert was preaching about life and death. What did you think?" He looked at me, smiled, and said, "From my perspective, when we get so close to knowing it might be near the end, it becomes the same for all of us. If you, Marie, think the important thing to do is go back to Indonesia and teach and help, do it fully with your whole heart and soul as well as you can. Now as I am growing close to saying good-bye to the world, there is still the same question and the same answer. My prayer is let me live life each day with an open heart and soul as well as I can."

I often reflect on how important his idea was. I loved Willy very much. After a month-long visit, I did return to Indonesia; about a year later, Willy went to heaven. I was in Indonesia on the day he died, and was invited to a big festival. I did not feel like going. I even said, "I think my brother has gone to heaven." It was intuition. At that time, we did not have phones or letters to send messages quickly. A few days or maybe a week later, a letter came from my father. He wrote that toward the end, Willy was barely speaking, but all of a sudden his voice became loud and clear. "Jesus, Mary and Joseph, I give you my heart, my body, and my soul." I do think that the very day Willy died, he was communicating by touching my heart in a special way. I felt his presence very strongly.

My brother Willy entertaining his nieces

Marie's sister Ann, her husband and their children, in Libya

Chapter 9

Turning Fear into Faith and Hope

In September 1965, a communist military coup overthrew President Sukarno and the Democratic Indonesian government, and it soon became a very dangerous environment for foreigners. In fact there were reports of people being kidnapped and tortured in gruesome ways. They told me I was on three targeted death lists. The mere thought was unnerving. I was taken to safety at an ex-official's home that night and I left soon after. Now I am grateful for all those who help me to escape. I alerted Grail and was given the option of waiting a few more weeks so I could fly to meet the president of Grail in France, but my decision was to leave right away. I boarded a plane to Libya, where my sister Ann, her husband, and two small children, sweet Joan and Charles, were waiting. After this traumatic ordeal, I really appreciated having time with my sister and family. I took solace during my stay with her, sitting on the banks of the Nile. Interestingly enough, a year later my sister and family had to be evacuated from Libya because of a similar situation. It was difficult to leave Indonesia so quickly without being able to say goodbye to my many colleagues, students, and friends.

What a tragedy, almost 1/2 million people were slaughtered: When will the politicians and world leaders ever learn???

"YOU CANNOT SIMULTANEOUSLY PREVENT AND PREPARE FOR WAR" Albert Einstein

What a welcome my parents and all my sisters and brothers gave me at the airport at midnight—hugs, tears, and kisses. I was back home to my family. I completed my master's degree at Stanford. I also had contracts with the Indonesian government so I was called back to Indonesia to translate after the coup. President Suharto was voted in. When I called home. I found out mom was in the hospital and needed long-term care, so I made the decision to return home to help mom. She had suffered a serious stroke. I lived with mom and Jose for over a year. It was a privilege to help my mother, as she had done so much for all of us.

Mom, your patience during the time after your stoke was amazing. What a blessing it was to share those days with you, and to help the family to take care of you. You and dad were the type of parents most children could only dream of. How grateful I am to both of you. During several of my difficult medical experiences, I was reminded of you, and tried to be strong and patience like you were. It is a mystery how you were able to do so many things in your life—raising twelve sons and six daughters, cooking, baking, gardening, sewing, and so much more. I fondly recall our family playing together on Sunday after church. There was softball, jumping rope, and fishing in our pasture's creek. You prepared many good meals of catfish and carp. You were so fast when you cleaned the fish! You baked many cakes and pies, and how you taught us how to make them, too. Imagine all the birthday cakes you made yearly for all eighteen of us. I fondly remember the many evenings we spent singing, especially on Sundays. You and dad would sing romantic songs and church hymns and German folk songs. Mom, did you enjoy that much as I did?

I remember how they described you in the newspaper article honoring you with an award from the pope!

The Award, presented to Anna Gertrude Mohr (1949)
Anna Gertrude Mohr is a saintly model Christian mother. She has devoted her life and talents to the formation of a Christian home. The quiet and unassuming mother is respected by her neighbors, esteemed by the parishioners of her parish and considered the outstanding mother of the parish and the countryside.

It makes me also remember the memorial of my beloved father, and how he was remembered.

Excerpt from Dad's eulogy given by Bishop Mark K. Carroll on December 20, 1968.

"A few days ago, our beloved friend, Peter Mohr, was called from this life to the radiant vistas of eternal life. His death created a great loss. In this rural area, Peter Mohr was an outstanding, successful farmer, a powerful good, both civic and religious. His death is a great loss to the Catholic Church, for he was a dedicated and devout member who edified all by his fidelity to his religious duties.

"Peter will have many reasons to expect a merciful judgment because he lived close to God and his family of eighteen children and

Marie's Journey of Love

thirty-six grandchildren—a special reason why the Lord will grant him the promise of eternal life. We can hear the Lord say, 'Well done, good and faithful servant. Enter thou into the joy of the Lord. Enter where nothing but love may enter and where love endures forever.'"

Bishop Mark Carroll gave the eulogy for both mom and dad.

Father, mother and Bishop Mark C. Carroll in our childhood home

The Fifth Smile of Our Lady

May 1949

Mrs. Anna Mohr

Mrs. Anna Mohr was born Anna Gertrude Strunk, daughter of Peter and Catherine Strunk, at St. Mark's March 4, 1901. She is married to Peter Mohr and to this happy couple came the blessing of 18 children.

Mr. and Mrs. Peter Mohr are a devoted Catholic husband and wife and loyal parishioners of St. Mark's parish. Most of the children are still at home. One daughter is a sister of the Order of St. Benedict, Guthrie, Okla., and a son, Clarence, is attending St. Gregory's college, Shawnee, Okla. Another son, Joe, is joining the Maryknoll Missioners as a lay brother. All have or are receiving their education at the parochial school of St. Mark's.

Anna Gertrude Mohr is a saintly, model Christian mother. She has devoted her life and talents to the formation of a Christian home. The quiet and unassuming mother is respected by her neighbors, esteemed by the parishioners of the parish, and considered the outstanding mother of the parish and the countryside. In spite of her busy days, Mrs. Mohr has always taken an active part in the women's societies of the parish and at present is an officer of the St. Mark Altar society.

Handwritten note:

My Mother received the Benemerente Medal from the Pope May 1949

Presented by Bishop Carrol in the Wichita Cathedral

Marie's Journey of Love

The Pearl Cruise

The Captain of the Pearl, my sister
Jose (Josephine), and me

Enjoying the cruise

54

Chapter 10

Cruising into New Adventures

A few months before mom died, the Indonesian publishers called and wanted me to finish a book I was working on in time for the annual Singapore Book Festival. I told mom I hated to leave her, but she said, "You've been here over a year. It was a very important and special time to have you here. If they want you to go, please go ahead. I'd like you to remember me when I was alive."

I was off to Indonesian again. The book, *The Call of the Hibiscus*, was published and approved during that time in Singapore. There was a dinner party in Jakarta, where I met the astronaut Gene Cernan.

After mom went to heaven, I stayed with my sister Jose. I was then hired for four months to be a lecturer on a cruise ship which sailed to countries in South East Asia. Someone at Stanford University had recommended me for the job. The cruise director interviewed me and signed me on right away. "We can only pay $1,000 a month," he said. "Fine," I replied. In my role as a lecturer, I spoke about each country's history, religion, and culture. The shore excursions would allow us to experience the country first hand. Seeing famous places brought life to the lectures I gave. There were twelve-course dinners and new sights and sounds. Indonesia offered some unusual experiences, including a visit to the island of Nias to see their special tribal dances. It was a healing time, given the loss I was still experiencing for my beloved mother. At night, I would go to the bow of the ship to see the glorious constellations clearly without interference from the city lights. The Southern Cross was awesome.

During the final month, I was able to invite my sister Jose to join me on the ship. She spent a month with me, including two weeks in Indonesia and two weeks in the other countries.

After four exciting months of cruising and lecturing were over and it was a year after mom's death, I was asked to return to Indonesia once again for the translation and editing of a book. After returning to United States, I resumed my job with the US State Department.

Whenever dignitaries came to Washington, I was flown there to interpret the Indonesian language for their spouses and business associates. Amazing experiences filled my life. After ten years of teaching Indonesian at Stanford University, it was exciting and challenging to be hired as an interpreter. This experience led me in a truly different direction in my life. I met some of the most amazing people during those years. I interacted with dignitaries from all over the world, including royal families, a woman who later became the President of Indonesia, Bill Clinton, who was governor at the time, and the list goes on. My experience in learning the Indonesian language had become the cornerstone for a career as a State Department interpreter and translation.

Gene Cernan, Astronaut and Marie 1987, Jakarta, Indonesia

Marie and Suljah take a ride in a betjak

Marie and friend contemplate the serenity of Buddha at the Borobudur, Mahayana Buddhist Temple in Magelang, Central Java, Indonesia

Marie's Journey of Love

Nias Island Dancers

Nias Island Jumper

Indonesian Government Conference

Book signing of Marie's book "Call of the Hibiscus"

Marie's Journey of Love

Chapter 11

The Road to Del

I was sad to hear that Netta, one of my teaching colleagues from Stanford, had passed. A dear friend told me there was to be a memorial service at the Stanford Memorial Church. Of course I attended the service, as I had always liked her very much. I noticed a child I assumed to be her precious little four-year-old granddaughter Jessica sitting on her grandpa Del's lap. She had beautiful blonde hair and blue eyes.

Marie in India ~ 1989

While talking with Kathryn, Del's sister, Jessica began pushing her way through the crowd. I was sure she was coming to see her Aunt Kathryn, but instead she reached up, looked at me, and declared, "You are my new nana." I was speechless and probably had a puzzled look on my face. She looked disappointed. "Don't you want to be my new nana? My other nana died and went to heaven." I looked at Kathryn; I could hardly believe what Jessica was saying. Down playing my surprise, I said, "But of course! Anyone would love to be your nana." I thought about the Big Brothers Big Sisters youth program; I'd did for years. I told Kathryn, "Wouldn't it be nice if she could select someone as her grandmother?" Jessica was getting a bit heavy, so I put her down, but to everyone who passed she would say, "This is my new nana" She held my hand as I gave my condolences to Del. He said, "Oh yes, I know who you are. You are Netta's friend who had been teaching in Indonesia."

I left to catch a plane to visit my family in Kansas, and then fly to Washington DC to attend a peace conference. I was still feeling quite mystified by my encounter with Jessica. When I returned home I sent a card to Del, which read, "If you don't mind, please send me your granddaughter Jessica's address. I want to keep in touch with her." Shortly after that I received a note from Del which read, "If you don't mind, I would also like to stay in touch with you." He shared that he had been talking with Kathryn, and she thought I would enjoy going to the annual Bing Crosby National Pro-Am golf tournament on the east coast. I was surprised, as I had only met Del once before the memorial service.

After the Washington D.C. peace conference, I had a trip planned to India. I had friends in Madras, India, and one in New Delhi who wanted me to take a side trip with her to Nepal. While I was traveling, Del sent many cards to my home.

Upon my return from this fascinating and wonderful journey, I was surprised to find that Del had sent a dozen red roses to welcome me home. I packed for the trip to meet him. His sister Kathryn was hoping I would come. Del said he and his granddaughter Jessica would greet me at the Dallas Airport, and from there, we would take another plane to North Carolina, where the tournament would be held. When I met them, Jessica threw her arms around my neck and said "Nana, nana"! Later, she continuously sang "Tea for Two" with her own versions of love words.

Kathryn arranged a beautiful suite at the hotel for she and I to share; Jessica and Del stayed in a room down the hall. Our days were filled with fun golf games, and in the evenings we would get decked out for the nightly dinner musical events. Jessica always came with us. In fact, she would not leave Del and me alone. One memorable moment after another brought Del and I closer towards our destiny. One evening, I requested a song from singer Gary Morris—a favorite of mine called, "Wind Beneath My Wings," which later became our song.

When we were finally alone, Del caught me off guard by saying, "I love you, Marie." I felt surprised and did not feel ready to say those words back to him. Early the next morning, there was a knock at the door. I turned over in my bed thinking it was someone for Kathryn, probably reporters or people coming in to do her makeup. But then the knock was on my door. I said, "It's okay, Kathryn. You can use the shower." I did not even open my eyes. The door opened very quietly and all of a sudden I sensed someone kneeling at my bed. There was Del, and he began proposing to me. I wish I had his words on tape; it was the most beautiful and poetic proposal a woman could ever want to hear. He said, "I told you that I love you. I don't say that lightly. For me it is not fifty percent; it is 100 percent and more." He shared many tender thoughts and said how beautiful he thought I was, both inside and out. Without hesitation, I said "Yes!" He suggested we tell Kathryn. I started thinking, *Dear God, I was not searching but I knew that when the right guy came along I would know it.* I had previously been involved with a Chinese man for a few years, but never felt ready to commit to him even though his desire had been to get married.

    I told Kathryn that I had agreed to marry her brother. She exclaimed, "He is such a good man, such a good man!" We hugged and cried. "I had always hoped that if I ever had a sister-in-law it would be someone like you or Netta," she said. We went on to finish our glorious week together, and on the weekend, Del announced our engagement to the guests. When we told Jessica, our biggest supporter, she asked "What does that mean for me?" I told her, "You'll now have both Netta and me as your nana. Now let me fix your hair and help you get dressed." Later that night, as she put up her hands to get her dress off, I said, "Now that it's just two of us here, what do you really think about us getting married?" She quickly burst out, "I'm so happy; Papa was so sad when nana died. I need your help so he will not feel so alone and sad."

    That night, at a family dinner, Del and I were asked when we would get married. Del said, "Week after next" We married nine days later. I told Del we must call Jose. I told her all about my week and what a great time I was having, and Del said he wanted to talk to her. He said, "I know Marie and I have not known each other long, but after this trip I feel like I have known her for a hundred years." I felt the same way. We told her about our upcoming marriage, and I said I did not want a big wedding. My prayer every day during the exciting days that followed was "Direct me, God. Show me the way."

Someone later asked if I ever doubted my decision to marry Del. I said no, this is it, this is the person I have waited for all my life. I was sixty years old and Del was sixty-four. Why wait? We wanted to be married in June before my family's annual Fourth of July reunion.

Del and I shared our story with Father John. After hearing our story, he said, "I feel this is true love, a marriage made in heaven." We had the wedding mass, and the reception was at my dear cousins Dr. Jim and Carol Lies's beautiful home overlooking Napa Valley. It was a small, lovely wedding of maybe thirty to forty people. Attending were some of my friends from Stanford, and my sister Jose and Del's sister Kathryn were our witnesses. We celebrated with them later during our annual family picnic. After our wondrous Mohr family and friend celebration, we went on to Texas to meet and celebrate with Del's father and relatives. They greeted us with open arms as well.

Marie and Del with granddaughter Jessica
(AKA the Golden Haired Messenger or Cupid)

Marie's Journey of Love

Marie, Kathryn Crosby Del's sister, and Del

Del, Marie and Bob Hope

Mary Francis Crosby, Harry Crosby and Marie

Marie's Journey of Love

Del and Marie – our wedding in Napa, CA – June 1989

Chapter 12

Our Magical New Life Together

Del had taken an early retirement to enjoy life while he was still healthy; I was still working and enjoying my job very much. Del did not have a problem with me continuing to work. I was still employed by the State Department, and could say yes or no to any of the contracts they offered. Usually we were not allowed to bring our spouses, but I had been doing this job since 1982. By then it was 1989 and my boss, Paul, said, "This time, Marie, you can bring your husband." From then on depending on the assignment, Del would accompany me.

My Del and Me – "...this is the person I have waited for all my life."

We flew to Nevada. Del and Netta had just purchased a house near Lake Tahoe before her illness took a turn for the worse.

My dear husband and I were most impressed by the magnificence of the lake and mountains near our house. Imagine how thrilled I was to settle in our new home.

Boxes were scattered all over the house, waiting to be unpacked. It was up to Del and me to set up the home. We started to unpack and decorate the house. Del said, "Now let's go on a honeymoon road trip to see the fall foliage in a variety of spectacular places." We planned to be gone for a month. Kathryn predicted that the trip would either make or break us—being newlyweds and together twenty-four hours a day, seven days a week.

Ever since he was a child, Del had loved to travel, and always dreamed of traveling around the world someday. He read a lot of travel magazines to plan his trip. Our month-long journey started in Canada. With travel planners helping us to organize our trip, we drove through United States to Nova Scotia, on to New York, and kept right on driving. We visited relatives from both sides whenever we were in their neck of the woods. I suggested we could attend an opera in Santa Fe. Del loved it and said, "Let's get tickets and come here every year!"

In fact, our lives together were woven with the memories of many special yearly events. There was the wonderful Mohr family annual picnic. There was also the Bing Crosby National Pro-Am golf tournament, which was an exciting time, mingling with famous movie stars. I can't fail to mention our yearly visits to precious Jessica, who brought Del and me together. We made many trips to California, and from Jessica's we often went on to visit many other friends. Kathryn, Del's sister, and Francis Ruth. Kathryn and Bing's lovely mansion was a favorite spot. We always received such a warm welcome. We claimed the mansion's green room as ours, and looked forward to staying there in Hillsborough, California

Del indulged his passion for travel by continually picking new places for us to visit. He was full of surprises. He would ask, "Marie, have you been to San Antonio?" If I said no, he would say, "Let's arrange a trip." Later he announced that the New Year's holiday would be celebrated in Tahiti. Later, we took a marvelous trip to Australia. Del's favorite was the African safari in Kenya. I especially loved our trip to Salzburg, Austria, mainly because of the music. Both of us loved Mozart, and even got to see his birthplace. You could attend concerts there any time of the year. Of course, Greece and Istanbul were also very interesting.

Besides travel, Del loved to garden, and he planted 200 rose bushes, a fruit orchard, and vegetable garden. He had worked for the chemical division of Texaco, and was always traveling in his job. He was a hard worker and a gentle man. His boss visited us twice after his retirement, and wrote in a letter that "In all the years Del worked for me, he never had a cross word for anyone. Everyone liked him. He had no enemies. He had a great sense of humor, Texas style."

We loved to lay on our lounge chairs on the deck and look up at the stars. We loved to hike, and drove into the mountains in his blue Jeep. He was an avid reader and always had several books in his suitcase. He was also a great whistler. We enjoyed our home near Lake Tahoe but, after a while, we got tired of the cold winters and decided to move to Arizona. We bought a lovely home on the golf course in 2000, but life has its twists and turns, and Del became ill.

Marie's Journey of Love

Marie interpreter for Indonesian Dignitaries – with then Arkansas Governor, Bill Clinton

*U.S. State Dept. in Washington, D. C., Del,
The Director of Language Interpreting, and Marie*

Del, Marie, and U.S. State Department Colleague

Marie and Del in Bali

Marie and Del, Mendocino, CA, Whale Watch

Marie's Journey of Love

Vacation and Adventures – my final years with Del

December: Sedona Red Rocks, Az.

January: S. Padre Island, Texas

Valentines Day: Canyon Lake, Az.

2003 Fun Trips

March: Grand Canyon, Az.

May: Bing Celebration Spokane Wa.

June: Kansas Wheatfields

Mohr Partnership meeting at 10 A.M. at Jose   Then down to the picnic grounds.

Wow, think that's a homerun Del! Hurry!

75

Marie's Journey of Love

Del and Marie at the piano in their Lake Tahoe Home

Del and Marie in Venice

Del and Marie visit the Borobudur Temple, Central Java

Del and Marie outside café in Vienna

November 2003 - Thanksgiving

Dear family and friends,

Happy Thanksgiving! Each day can be a celebration of Giving Thanks. There is so much to be grateful for. Each day is graced with gifts, if only our hearts are open to every moment.

Del and I have experienced years of great joy and happiness. We have enriched each other's lives. He gave me grandchildren; I gave him brothers. He embraced the Catholic faith shortly after our marriage, a profound gift. We have had many great travel adventures abroad and here, visiting family and friends, admiring the wonders of God's creation. Those were the joyful days of "Wine and Roses." Most of all, a life filled with profound mutual love. Yes, truly, "To love and be loved is the greatest gift on earth."

Our love deepens as we face a new challenge to continue life's journey, not by choice but by circumstance. Mid July, Del was hospitalized for some weeks. It was determined that a "Memory Care Facility" was the necessary step to provide him with the best care and safety. It's a joy to see his face light up with a welcome smile when I come daily to visit him. This is our life now and we embrace it, yes, the pain with the joy, the thorns with the roses. Our love, faith and support of family and friends will carry us through the difficult days ahead. All else may fade, but "Love is forever."

In closing we wish you Peace filled holidays - Holy Days for each of you and your families. We pray for Global Peace in our suffering war torn world of today. Keep us in your thoughts and prayers.

With love,

Del and Marie

Chapter 13

Saying Good-bye to Del

The Memorial Mass for Del, in Prince of Peace Church, was beautiful. Father John, our former pastor from Nevada, and our priest officiated. A choir with their harmonious voices created a peaceful loving atmosphere. We had a harpist and trumpeter. Kathryn gave a beautiful eulogy. Part of her sharing included a very touching song, "All the Things You Are" Many of our family and friends came from far and near.

Sometime later, Mike, a friend of mine, walked me to my car. He shared that there are often signs from our loved ones after they die. It was Christmas day, and I turned on the radio to hear some beautiful Christmas music. The song playing was called "Going Home." I began to cry. It seemed to be a message from Del. I needed some reassurance and this song gave it to me. Thank you Del.

The years with my wonderful husband were truly a treasured gift. Lord, are you pleased with my life's journey? Of course, it still continues now. After all, I am only eighty years young. Thank you, dear Lord, for walking the path of life with me. I ask you to embrace me forever.

A Memorial Celebration of the Life of Delbert E. Grandstaff, JR.

Eventide

Walking hand in hand we visit the sanctuary of Mozart and gift the forest
With the blossom of our passion

The morning blush and eventide we have created plays on
~~ sauntering the moons of all the planets
Caressing the shores and enveloping our song

No matter the state of our shadow's union
We are always there together at the first light of dawn
Watching the birds dance about the bath

Hand in hand we hear the whisper of dusk
And celebrate the christening of our laughter

We weave a brilliant tapestry ~~ blending air and ether with ever after...

Together on the beaches we will always walk~~ with the sound of our souls
Echoing in the conch shells and embracing the halo on our brow
We take in the blessing and gently bow

Knowing that angels lead and surround our sacred path
And joy and faith will leave us never

For we will walk together in the wisdom and
fortune of the golden haired messenger
Greeting the eventide...

We will swim this ocean undivided
Our love and devotion will live on forever...

"TO LOVE IS TO LIVE FOREVER"

Delbert E. Grandstaff

Date of Birth: September 16, 1926

Date of Entrance into Eternal Life: December 23, 2003

Memorial Celebration: January 24, 2004
12:00 Noon
Prince of Peace Church, Sun City West, Arizona

Celebrant: Father John Corona
Con Celebrant: Father Michael Minogue

Combined Choirs

Director of Liturgy and Music: Michael J. McGraw

Organist:	David Mueller
Piano:	Jeanne Campbell
	Steve Gold
Keyboard:	Liz Manske
Violin:	Eileen Brown
Trumpet:	Bill Fedor
Harpists:	Sherry Cook
	Joyce Buekers

You are invited to join the family at the home of Del and Marie after the service.
18011 N. Timber Ridge Drive
Sun City Grand, Arizona

Mass of The Resurrection

Prelude: Harp in the Church Gathering area
Ave Maria

Urn Bearer & Attendants
Grandchildren: Jessica, David, and Kayla

Gathering: Joyful, Joyful We Adore Thee

First Reading: Creation Will Be At Peace (Choir) from Isaiah

Psalm: Psalm 42: 2-3, 43: 4-5 ~ Read by Margo Roy
My Soul Is Thirsting For the Living God,
When Shall I See Him Face to Face

Second Reading: Romans 8: 14-23 ~ Read by Dr. John Mohr

Gospel Acclamation: Celtic Alleluia

Gospel: John 14: 1-6 ~ Father John Corona
Homily: Father John Corona

General Intercessions: Denise Mohr

Presentation: How Great Thou Art
Gift Bearers: Josephine and Nancy Mohr

Communion: Harp Solo
Amazing Grace ~ Organ & Trumpet
(Choir in vs. 3)

Eulogy: Kathryn Crosby
All The Things You Are

Final Commendation: May The Angels Lead You To Paradise

Sending Forth: City Of God

Like The Wind

Time will never erase
What God has blessed us with

In the midst of what remains ~ I know I will never really lose you
I will be by your side forever
A mantle of eternity ~ for you to treasure
Loving you forever

I will be there cloaking your wishes
Cherishing your passion ~ in the silence and flow
Embracing your shadow and soul

When you least anticipate in the tumble of your day
I will move the leaves on the trees and make the blossoms sway

As you walk your destined path I will cause the flutter on your way
Wherever you turn I will be there ~ loving you forever
Reminding you ~ of the enchantment and sacredness
The wind brings to your life

I will always be by your side
Enveloping the silent places where only moonlight peers
The dark and lonely pockets ~ when you face your fears
I will be there ... like a spirit surrounding you ... transcending your prayers ...

Like the wind ~ the blustery caress of my love will come again
Beyond the sunrise and sunset
You will never, ever forget
The delicate fragrance and cadence of my love

Like the wind ~ moving your aura and wisdom
I will never leave you
Will always be your lover and your friend
Imparting breezes forever ...
Like the wind my love for you will never end ...

Poetry dedicated to Del & Marie Grandstaff
By Lesa Caldarella

"Healing – Harmony & Flowering"

A dear friend, Lesa from Phoenix, knew my husband's health condition required hospice care. She phoned and said, "What time would it be convenient for me to come and visit you and Del? I have a surprise gift for you."

She arrived at the agreed upon time and we met in the courtyard garden. With her was a lovely blond carrying a harp! It was a harpist, Joyce Buekers, the founder of The Harp Foundation. Her beauty and harp music permeated the space around us. This moment of therapeutic harp music and new friendship entered my heart forever! Del, my beloved husband, was tightly grasping my hand, always a sign of pain. Gradually he relaxed and became so peaceful, his pain level decreased. The music touched my soul deeply, a flood of tears poured forth, releasing the pain and grief in my heart. How helpless we feel when unable to do more to relieve the suffering of those we love.

Before Joyce and Lesa left, I asked if someone could play the harp in my husband's room once a week. They told me Sherry Cook played for The Harp Foundation and was at Sun Health Hospice. We arranged for her to play each Tuesday in my beloved Del's room for the final months of his life here on earth.

The day before Christmas Eve, a Tuesday, the hospice nurse told me, "Del will have only a few more days with us." Our Christmas tradition was to attend or listen to Handel's "Messiah." Holding his hand, we listened to the complete CD of this beautiful oratorio. I fed him an ice cream shake, the last food he was able to eat. He opened his eyes, looked at me and said, "I love you!" His last words here on earth.

A knock at the door, Sherry, the harpist, "Do you still want me to play? I have the song you requested last week." "Please come in," I said, and she began to play Bach's "Jesus Joy of Man's Desiring." While embracing my beloved, the room filled with this sacred music, his spirit left his body – his breath taken up in the breath of God. His transition was so peaceful, so serene. What a grand finale for Del!

Seven years of my life were spent in Indonesia. At the time of death in a family, friends say, "Your loved one has gone home to God," — "Kekasihmu, pulang Ke Rahmat tul'Allah." Yes, my beloved has gone home to God and awaits to welcome me.

This magical harp story came full circle during the Memorial Celebration of Del's life at Prince of Peace Church. Harp, violin, trumpet and choir music graced the Mass. After the service, more than 70 friends and family came to our home for sharing and dinner. Dear Joyce greeting the guests with heavenly harp music as they entered the front door of our home.

(continued on back)

A new circle of events was to follow. Del's spirit whispered in my heart, "Why don't you try to play the harp?" A truly new and novel idea. Maybe someday to join the Angel Harp Choir in heaven, but now? Well, why not? I rented a harp for three months. Sherry, my teacher was most encouraging. "You're doing great," she remarked. Again Del whispers in my heart, "May 19, a perfect birthday gift for you!" Yes, I now have a harp. What a birthday present!

A new circle of events with the harp is now taking birth. Upon receiving a generous inheritance from my dear mother and father, I decided to honor them and in memory of my beloved Del to give a donation to The Harp Foundation. This was to begin the "Angel Song" therapeutic harp program at Sun Health Del E. Webb Hospital, where Del and I have received excellent care in the past years. The harp, one just like mine, was blessed and brought to the hospital on May 19. Yes, this time a birthday gift from me for the many people whose lives will be touched by the healing, heavenly strings of the harp music. May it become for all, as it has been for me, a message, a gift of "healing, harmony and flowering."

—Marie Mohr-Grandstaff
2008

THE HARPFOUNDATION
Transforming and touching lives

(602) 265-4014
www.theharpfoundation.org
info@harpfoundation.org

Sun Health

Sun Health Del E. Webb Hospital

(623) 876-5432
www.sunhealth.org

The Harp Foundation Proudly Presents

Sun Health Del E. Webb Hospital's
"Angel Song"
Therapeutic Harp Program

Graciously donated
By Del & Marie Grandstaff

THE HARP FOUNDATION
Transforming Lives and Healing Hearts

The Angel Song Program

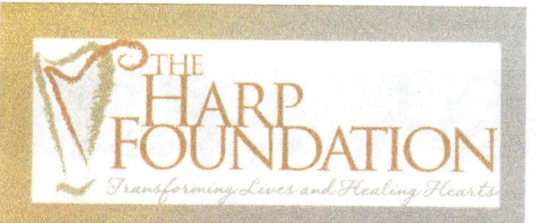

Marie Grandstaff

Because of the Grandstaffs:

- Marie and her beloved husband Del Have funded the therapeutic Angel Song harp program and purchased the program's harp

- Harpists play at patient's bedsides, offering soothing and healing moments at Banner Del E. Webb Hospital through the Angel Song Program

- infants, children, adults and their families benefit from harp music during stressful hospital stays

"Marie has touched our hearts with her selfless generosity and kind spirit,...We are so fortunate to be the recipient for the Angel Song Program" says a hospital administrator

Marie's Journey of Love

Happy Birthday Marie

Marie accepting gift from Del Webb Hospital presented by Joan Simon

Marie and Dr. Pozun her cardiologist and a speaker at the dedication of the Angel Song Program

Marie's Journey of Love

Marie presenting harp to Joan Simon of Banner Del Webb Hospital

Marie with Reverend Joyce Buekers Founding Director of the Harp Foundation who is blessing the Harp for the Angel Song program

Chapter 14

Love of Music

My interest in music continued to be nurtured through my involvement in the church choir. I was also involved in the Wichita Choral Society. What a thrill when, at Christmas time, with the symphony, they sang Handel's *Messiah*. One unforgettable season, we performed Mendelssohn's *Elijah*. I still smile when I recall the purity of the young boy's solo. Music is a true nourishment of the spirit!

All my life, I have kept that profound love and passion for music. Although I did not pursue music studies, the magic of my life has given me many wonderful opportunities to experience music.

As a gift, after our crops were harvested, dad and mom bought us a piano. I taught myself how to play songs for our family's sing-along sessions. Several of my sisters also played. Dr Joe Mohr, my nephew, is an astrophysicist, researcher, and professor in Munich, Germany. When I told him I was writing this book, he sent me a letter titled "Memories of Aunt Marie" (see appendix). In it, he wrote,

My first memories of Aunt Marie are at the piano. She could captivate an entire room full of aunts, uncles, and cousins with her piano playing and singing. Even though I was young, I understood that

Aunt Marie was gifted. She taught herself to play. Wow! She could listen to any song on the radio and just sit down and play it on the piano. Double wow!

Joe went on to talk about how supportive I was to any of them who took an active interest in music, and how I inspired and amplified his interest and dedication to his music. He also shared that "Aunt Marie also plays the accordion." He volunteered the idea that the accordion possesses an enjoyable yesteryear kind of quality. My father had encouraged me to play piano and accordion. He loved classical music.

My only formal study of music was in the 1960s at Grailville, and recently harp lessons. As I approached my eightieth birthday, I look back at all the memorable events that have presented themselves to me. There was the beauty of the Gregorian chant and folk music. Later, when I was on the island of Java, I joined a group of university students in Surabaja. We learned to play the wonderful Javanese gamelan, a musical ensemble from Indonesia, typically from the islands of Bali or Java, featuring a variety of instruments such as metallophones, xylophones, kendang or drums, and gongs, bamboo flutes, and bowed and plucked strings.

How excited we were when asked to play for the radio station in Surabaja.

Such sweet memories! On to California in the 1970s, where I joined a Bach chorus. At Christmas, we performed Handel's *Messiah* at the beautiful, modern St. Mary's Cathedral in San Francisco. Other programs were held in Berkeley and surrounding areas. Later I had the joy of singing with the Stanford chorus. One glorious finale was Beethoven's Ninth Symphony, with the San Francisco Symphony.

The major chapter of my music journey took place not long ago. At the age of seventy-five, I decided to take harp lessons. I was introduced to therapeutic harp music by Lesa and Joyce during my husband's illness. I was deeply moved by its healing effect, and that inspired me to learn. Music has truly been for me a gift of Healing, Harmony, and Flowering.

Marie practicing her harp in her home

Marie, Dr. Gladys McGarey, and Joyce Buekers
Banner Del Webb Hospital

David Ice, Harpist playing at the St. Vincent de Paul "Restoring Hope" program

Marie's Journey of Love

Marie in Sedona with young harp enthusiast

Alla Yashneva, harpist

Jaxen age 6, Marie's grandnephew playing harp

Sedona Harp Program, Marie with child on her lap

Marie's Journey of Love

Sedona Harp retreat, Adrienne Bridgewater, harpist playing a song dedicated to Marie and Dr. Gladys McGarey

Marie at Harp Foundation event telling her "harp story" with Joyce Buekers, Founding Director of the Harp Foundation

Chapter 15

A Twist of Fate and Two Close Calls!

Here are two of the incidents that came so close to ending my life here on earth. First, my cardiac arrest and then a stroke..

One day I declined an invitation from friends to go to an evening of music at the West Valley Museum. At approximately five o'clock in the morning, I had an urge to go to the bathroom and discovered I was too weak to even get out of bed. I decided to slowly slide down to the floor. Well, that was the finish. There was no way to get myself up, and I was now on the opposite side of the bed from our phone. What a terrible situation to be in. Now I had to figure out how to reach the phone! Inch by inch, I struggled to get myself around the bed. The thoughts going through my mind were many. I thought perhaps if I could lay flat or sleep for a bit, I would be stronger. Every time I would start to do that, a deep voice in my spirit said, If you sleep, you will never wake up again. The urge to survive was stronger than just giving up. I was talking to Del, saying, "Yes, it is my seventy-seventh year, the same age you were when you went to heaven. But it is not my time yet."

From Sunday at five o'clock in the morning until the same time on Monday, I lay there. Eventually I somehow dragged my body along the bedroom floor and finally reached the phone stand. I pulled the cord and was able to pull the telephone down on the floor. When the answer came, it was a wrong number. Then I pushed the 0. The operator said, "Where are you, dear?" I answered, "I am on the floor, please don't hang up." She replied, "I am calling 911." That is what saved my life. She was truly an angel. Within about five minutes, the EMTs came. Thank God one of my windows was not locked and they were easily able to get in. They found me still on the floor, too weak to stand up. Two kind men helped me up very gently. Imagine my wonder—I could walk to the bathroom with help. Another surprise—my answers were all coherent. One of the EMTs said, "Bring the stretcher and take her to the ambulance."

Dear Dodie came to the hospital and she stayed until they took me to my room. There were tests—an MRI, CAT scan, and others. Yes, it was a cardiac arrest caused by some medications. During the first stop at Banner Del E. Webb Medical Center, a gentle nurse sponge-bathed me and then asked, "Do you want anything, my dear?" I said, "Oh yes, please call this number." Extremely weak, I was still able to recall her Margo's number.

I don't remember much after that, only that after the test, I was rushed to Banner Boswell Medical Center in an ambulance. Then there was immediate surgery to implant a pacemaker. Can you imagine? It was a St. Jude pacemaker! Awakening after the surgery the following day, it was like seeing an angel standing near me while they wheeled me back to the room. There she was—Margo, my dearest sister. She and her husband live in Texas. Imagine Margo arriving immediately the second day.

She stayed with me for two weeks. She came every morning, and we shared dinner. We did pray—whoops, of course we did, but I meant to say "play" Scrabble. I wanted to be assured that I was still able to use my brain. We had a good time. Words can't say how grateful I am for that precious sister. Thank you, mom and dad, for welcoming this beautiful baby into our family, the eighteenth child. Now she is a nurse.

My sister Denise had returned from Tulsa, and she came to visit and brought some delicious meals to my home. Dear Dr. Pozun continued to care for me. He said that it was safe to travel since I had made an original plan to celebrate with a sisters' trip—a river cruise called autumn leaves. How wonderful that the four of us came—Jose from Kansas, Theresa from Maryland, Margo from Texas, and me from Arizona. What a precious time we had. The other two sisters declined, but this time with my three sisters was very special, almost like a sacred event in my life. I think it was a celebration of being back among the

Standing in front of the Mississippi, my sister Theresa on our "sisters' trip

Margo, Theresa, Marie, and Jose on the "sisters' trip" river cruise

living after the cardiac arrest episode.

November 1 to 15, 2008 I was a patient in Banner Del E. Webb Medical Center. I had suffered a serious stroke. I had been recuperating from a four-day eye clinic. It took three hours that evening to reach the kitchen phone. I was able to call James and Christel, who have truly become family to me. Thank God they were home. I mustered the strength to say "Emergency!" They quickly came and knelt beside me on the floor. I was suddenly very peaceful. I said, "Oh, Christel, you are here just in time for me to say thank you and to say good-bye to all my family and friends. Angels are taking me to heaven—Del is calling me." Christel kept saying, "It's not yet your time."

James had called 911, and soon two gentle guys put me on a cot and took me off to the hospital. They visited me daily for a few days before going back to Germany.

Joyce Buekers visited me at the hospital with a dozen beautiful red roses. She also brought along a small harp. I tried to play it, and found the sounds to be very soothing. What a blessing! I had helped introduce the harp program "Angel Song" to the hospital. Now I was to be the recipient of the program. We never know where our path will take us. Thank You Jesus! Our hearts and lives must be open to whatever the Lord will bring.

The sixth day Christel and James had to return to Germany, and my dear friends Barbara and Jim came and helped me at the hospital. By the time I was moved to the therapy section, I was longing to see some of my sisters. It had been suggested that they wait until I was ready to go home. Margo came the day before, and was a great help with paperwork and in preparing things at home, including making delicious chicken noodle soup. It was still difficult for me, and I had to eat very slowly. Then, a big surprise! Theresa, my sister, walked in the door of our home! We celebrated and enjoyed a number of games, including Scrabble. Too soon, it was time for them to leave. They helped arrange for four therapists to come to my home.

Dr. Pozun, my cardiologist, said, "The most important therapy that you can do daily is this—play the harp or play the piano faithfully for half an hour each day." So I did. I firmly believe that the harp vibrations from this heavenly instrument heals. It helps both the right and left hemispheres of the brain. I am so grateful to the dear friends and doctors. How blessed I am. Linda helped with light soup suppers and stayed with me all night until after our light breakfast was served. Almost every afternoon for several weeks, dear Dianne came to check in on me and visit.

Jose came and spent Christmas and New Year's with me.

Dec 26 was the beautiful Cook family concert in our home. Five

The talented Cook Family gave a lovely Christmas performance in my home

lovely children and mom and dad entertained us with beautiful music on the harp, French horn, tuba, heavenly music on the flute and, of course, the piano. The concerts and music in our lovely home truly blessed us.

The best book to help me after the stroke was Jill Bolte Taylor's book My Stroke of Insight. I learned so much about the beauty and complexity of the brain. Yes, there are truly fresh insights for any person who studies and reads this book.

I continue to live to the fullest, and fill my life with many special moments with friends and family. I continue to take trips to Kansas, California, Santa Fe, and in Arizona.

Dr. Michael Esber is my new friend, as are his wife and children. One weekend they invited me to become the godmother of their sweet two-year-old son. They adopted him as an infant. What an interesting ceremony. Michael is from Lebanon, and so the event was held at the St. Joseph Maronite Catholic Church here in Phoenix. They had a great feast, all Lebanese food, plus a big birthday cake. We became special friends after I played the harp in one of his patients' rooms. The beauty and healing music of the harp inspired and moved him. I played the harp as a volunteer for the The Harp Foundation's Angel Song Program.

I also continued to play the harp and piano at community locations, including a local memory care home. About thirty patients sing familiar songs and enjoy the sing-a-long hour.

As long as I live, I will try and do good and help others whenever and wherever I can.

I am here to be helpful.
I am here to represent You who sent me.
I do not have to worry about what to say or what to do, because You who sent me will direct me.
I am content to be wherever You wish, knowing You are there with me.
I will be healed as I let You teach me to heal.

Author unknown

Marie's Journey of Love

Chapter 16

Celebration from Birth to Rebirth

My eightieth birthday, what a landmark! It has been truly full of blessings beyond words. Friends from around the world called to send greetings. Dr. Eric from Russia, Baidy from the Philippines, Daisy from Indonesia, Pat and June from Australia, Susan, back from China. Many people reached out to send their love via mail or phone. All were personal messages, not emails that click out and send the same message to fifty or hundred people with the exact same news. I treasured the care and kindly words that arrived and my heart was filled with gratitude. Alla, a dear Russian friend and a very talented concert harpist, came over with her husband and prepared a special Russian meal. Many of these people who are in my life are from the adventures during my years with Grail, and numerous others are from Stanford University. Several of my brothers and sisters are perhaps the closest to me, and they also sent their greetings. We share such a special bond from the days of my birth and childhood. Mom and dad hold a very important place in my life, from birth until this very day. I call on them in heaven for help. "Now that you are near me to help guide me, can I ever thank you, my dear parents, for all the love you gave me I admire you, respect and

Marie's Journey of Love

rejoice and celebrate you."

Our four-year-old cherub Jessica is grown up and now she has her own family. Their little boys are precious, my four grandsons, River, Skyler, Hunter and Phoenix.

My granddaughter Jessica (the Golden Hair Messenger), with me on her wedding day

Jessica and Jeremy – Mrs. and Mr. Sherman on their wedding day

Jessicas' twins, River and Skyler with their Nana enjoying the music

A Few Concluding Thoughts

Deep gratitude to all of you, my dear family and friends, for all the care and love you have and still give me.

I have been inspired by the writings by Henri Nouwen over the years. I will conclude this with the following piece he wrote, "Love Deeply." It is a fitting finale from my heart to all of you.

> *"Marie's Journey of Love"*
> *Love Deeply*

LOVE DEEPLY

Do not hesitate to love and to love deeply. You might be afraid of the pain that deep love can cause. When those you love deeply reject you, leave you, or die, your heart will be broken. But that should not hold you back from loving deeply. The pain that comes from deep love makes your love ever more fruitful. It is like a plow that breaks the ground to allow the seed to take root and grow into a strong plant. Every time you experience the pain of rejection, absence, or death, you are faced with a choice. You can become bitter and decide not to love again, or you can stand straight in your pain and let the soil on which you stand become richer and more able to give life to new seeds.

The more you have loved and have allowed yourself to suffer because of your love, the more you will be able to let your heart grow wider and deeper. When your love is truly giving and receiving, those whom you love will not leave your heart even when they depart from you. They will become part of your self and thus gradually build a community within you.

Those you have loved deeply become a part of you. The longer you live, there will always be more people to be loved by you and to become part of your inner community. The wider your inner community becomes, the more easily you will recognize your own brother and sisters in the strangers around you. Those who are alive within you will recognize those who are alive around you. The wider the community of your heart, the wider the community around you. Thus the pain of rejection, absence, and death can become fruitful. Yes, as you love deeply the ground of your heart will be broken more and more, but you will rejoice in the abundance of the fruit it will bear.

Copyright© 1996 by Henri J. M. Nouwen. From *THE INNER VOICE OF LOVE*, published by Doubleday. This broadside was created to honor the life and teachings of Henri Nouwen, a dear friend of Ken Aman's.

Marie's Journey of Love

Addendums

Part I. Thoughts, Reflections, and Tributes from Marie's Friends and Family

Dear Marie

It is good to know you are doing your memoirs. Your life experiences <u>need</u> to be recorded and will be of interest to many; not only family members, but also your friends and many others.

I am in awe of your accomplishments! You have had a variety of experiences; going to Grailville, getting your college education in New York, living in *and a master deg from Stanford Univ.* Indonesia, escaping a Revolution, teaching at Stanford and working for the State Department, which could fill a book. In addition your have the experience of growing up in Kansas in a family of eighteen children surrounded by loving parents and myriads of relatives. Also, marrying Del Grandstaff and living in Nevada then moving to Arizona. The role of music in your life seems like an over arching umbrella to all your experiences.

Denise, Catherine Mohr

Marie's oldest sister, Dence

Marie's Journey of Love

I remember the very few times she visited like it was yesterday. Aunt Marie used to visit our home in Wichita when she was home to see family. We really enjoyed each other's company when I was very little. The last time she visited she got me a wishing well that I still use today. I've made plenty of wishes that have been wished many times before, for her to come back and visit me again. When Marie first started playing the harp, she would play it for me over the phone. She sounded like an angel on the harp. When I was 6, Aunt Marie bought me a harp that was just my size and I took lessons for about a year until I broke my arm. It was a very hard instrument to play, but I still listen to harp music when I go to bed. It makes me think of Aunt Marie and my guardian angels who are always with me.

- Jaxen McPhail, 11 yr old great nephew (age 5 in pictures)

How we met wonderful Marie Grandstaff

It is exactly twenty year ago when we were visiting friends in Minden, Nevada, coming from Germany on vacation.

We attended holy Mass at St. Galls Church in Gardnerville. During that wonderful Mass, the priest, Father John, asked who is visiting from out of town. A lot of people raised their hands and so did I. When I was asked to speak I said we are from Germany.

A lot of people welcomed and greeted us after Mass and is how we met our dear Marie and her beloved husband Del. We had a long talk and they mentioned that they are going on trip to Europe two months later. Of course, we invited them to come to see us, which they did and this was the beginning of our wonderful relationship.

We had visited each other many times and after they moved to Arizona, we came to see them again, of course. We always had a wonderful time together. They were the reason for our moving into Sun City Grand which we both call home. We love it very much to be here, especially since we have Marie here.

We have a lot to be thankful for, especially to have met her.

Our relationship has become so close that we call each other sister and brother. We hope to be together with our dear Marie

for a long time to come and we pray that our Lord blesses her and us with health and happiness.

Your sister and brother Christel and James Blum

May 2013

My Nana, Marie, is someone I will always thank God for. She came into my Pop Pop's and my life in a dark hour and turned the lights back on. I will always remember asking her, at the memorial service of my grandma, if she will be my new nana. Little did I know, at the age of four, that she would soon be a part of our family. We touched each others hearts then and still do today, almost 25 years later.

Nana has been there for me through it all. Her loving and compassionate nature towards others made it easy to confide in her with the pains and joys of life. She has been a role model to so many and has accomplished so much, but most importantly to me, she loved my PopPop with all her heart and I couldn't have hoped for anything more. The love between them still echos within me and I only hope to love my husband and children the same way. I will be forever grateful to God for sending such a special and unique person to stand as an ever blooming flower in our garden of love.

Jessica Shuman
5/2013

Mother Marie came into my life when I was 18 years old and traveling in Europe with my harp instructor. Marie and her precious husband, Del and I spent hours touring, talking, laughing and learning. I felt so loved and accepted and genuinely cared for by this dear couple. Marie became my mother that week and we formed a bond that has spanned decades. When my own beloved mother passed away a few years later, Mother Marie continued to guide and comfort me, especially during a challenging time of grieving and rearing 8 children. Her wisdom in family relationships, how to really love your husband and what true faith in God is continues to inspire and challenge me. What joy it brought me personally when Mother began taking harp lessons. We played together one day in our home and it was a dream come true- a mother and daughter playing in harmony! Mother Marie continues to motivate me with her giving spirit and the aura of peace and joy her life reflects. I am truly honored to know Marie Mohr Grandstaff and to be called her DAUGHTER.

Crystal W. Twibell
Glennville, Georgia

Marie and Crystal at the harp

Memories of Aunt Marie...

~~Below~~ I have written down my memories of Marie in chronological order. I hope these are helpful and that they can be incorporated in part into Aunt Marie's story.

Memories from Boyhood

My first memories of Aunt Marie are of her at the piano. She could captivate an entire room full of aunts, uncles and cousins with her piano playing and singing—and the rooms were always full at Grandma's house in Wichita! Even though I was very young, I understood that Aunt Marie was gifted. I remember telling my Dad how amazed I was, and how he related the stories of his sister Marie's youth—in particular, I remember "She taught herself to play." (wow!) and "She could listen to any song on the radio and just sit down and play it on the piano." (double wow!)

Many of the Mohr grandkids played instruments- in particular the piano- and I was one of those. Aunt Marie took a special interest in us all. She tried to encourage us with our playing and was always so supportive. She would always ask us to play something for her. As we packed for our long trips to Wichita, my Mom would always say "Better take your piano books" if Aunt Marie was going to be there. I think back now, and I understand that my playing was nothing particularly special, but Aunt Marie's interest somehow amplified my interest and dedication to my music, and I suspect it was the same for all of us!

Aunt Marie also plays the accordion. To me, this particular instrument has a "yester-year" quality- the notes suggest the piano but the accordion brings with it the atmosphere of a folk festival. Everyone would smile when Aunt Marie played the accordion. I remember talking with her about her accordion one quiet afternoon- she showed me how to play a few notes, but the accordion was huge and dwarfed my small frame. She asked me to wait a moment and dug into her things and returned with a small accordion- perfect for a child! I was thrilled, of course! She let me borrow that instrument for a few months, and I tried to play it in a dedicated fashion. But it was too much for me as a young boy (I don't have the same gifts that Aunt Marie has), and I brought it back to Wichita on the next trip. Still, it was a big event for me to have been entrusted with that accordion for several months!

Memories from the Teen Years:

As I grew older I began to appreciate the complexity of the relationships in Kansas. The Mohr family is unusually large, and the uncles and aunts were born over a broad span of time between the mid 20's and the mid 40's. While all siblings shared the same physical environment of the Colwich farm and surrounding farm families, they developed individual world views that reflect the wide range that one might expect from a mid-American farm family with 18 kids! Marie has a strikingly positive attitude toward the world. She is a big dreamer, and it seems she sometimes sees the world as she wills it to be, even if there may be some small details that don't quite conform to her will! She was different in this respect from the other family members—indeed from most of the other people I have ever met.

To me as a young teen her attitude embodied the ideal Christian view of the world. She seemed to see only the positive in people, and to be guided by a purity of vision that was unique. My own view as a young man evolved over time- ultimately I developed a tendency to sense not only the positive but also the negative in the world around me. Nevertheless, in my interactions with Aunt Marie I felt a calling to the world of the positive and the pure. She seemed to pursue a world of thought that reflected the tenets of the New Testament. And she successfully lived this life, too!

Memories from the College Years:

Aunt Marie and I stayed in contact through the college years. I went quite a distance to attend school in Boston (at MIT), and her support was very important to me, as was the support of the rest of my family and friends. Once my future wife Amy and I visited her in New York City during one of her trips as a translator for an international visitor. During my graduation she came to Boston to spend a couple of days. It meant the world to me to have her there. I remember she gave me the book that she said reflected her world views- *The Phenomenon of Man* by Tielhard de Chardin. We talked late into the night, and she revealed to me some of her experiences that made clear that God is very real in this world. Aunt Marie has always been a very spiritual person, and this is something I respect deeply. I came away from her visit determined to find this spirituality in my own life, but then I moved on to graduate school and found myself consumed by the details of my studies. I have remained open to such experience as those related by Aunt Marie, but so far I have not been blessed by any such events. I remain watchful to this day.

Recent Memories:

Amy and I named our second daughter Emily Marie Mohr in honor of Aunt Marie. Emily has grown to be a very powerful spirit much like her Great Aunt, but at least at this point has not found her way to the same spiritual peace! ☺ Marie visited us once in our home in Urbana, Illinois. It was an amazing visit! We spent three or four days at the piano as Marie played song after song. I have memories of a Sunday morning with us all there in our pajamas singing and enjoying the wonderful music that Marie was making on the piano. It was a beautiful experience for us all, and I cherish it especially for my daughters Elizabeth and Emily. Since then Elizabeth has devoted herself to the piano and is doing well. Emily has taken lessons but has drifted away again. Just today she spent time playing her old songs on the piano, and I cannot help thinking that the strong spirit of her Aunt Marie is still pushing her in this direction. I hope Marie is successful where Amy and I as parents have failed! ☺

Overview:

All told these are personal experiences that I expect were repeated many times among others that Aunt Marie has touched. She has served as a sort of shining beacon of positivity, righteousness and love in my life. I haven't found it within myself to follow her as closely as I know I should have, but her example has had a deep impact on my life, as I'm sure it has on many others. She is a beautiful person and a strong spirit—in the Mohr family—and I imagine in the broader world as well. She has followed a fascinating path through life that includes many travels, exposure to foreign cultures and dedication to a spiritual life. I love her deeply and treasure her uniqueness. I hope to see it flow through the lives of my daughters.

Joe Mohr (born 23.02.1968, Marie Mohr's nephew) *Astro Physicist in Munich, Germany*

Nancy Mohr – Phy. Therapist at Children's Day in Kansas City, Ka
(Marie's god-mother)

My godmother Marie is my aunt, and dear friend. This started 46yrs ago when she committed to being my godmother (thank you mom & dad!). As a child, I looked forward to her Christmas present every year, because even if she wasn't present, she always made sure there was a gift for me under the Mohr's Christmas tree ☺! Her gifts were exceptional – always unique & usually from a different country. The best thing about them - was the sweet note that *always* accompanied the gift. She would tell me where she was and what she was doing, and always had words of support and gratitude for me. I would wonder how she knew me, since she lived out of town. Marie didn't have to know me *well* – in order to give me her support; she simply had faith in me!

In the last 20yrs or so, we've become dear friends. I feel very blessed to have her in my life. As a pre-teen, I and my family visited her in CA (my first time seeing the ocean). And when I was in my 30's, I visited her and Del in Nevada. More recently, I've visited her several times in Phoenix. This last time was very memorable, as I managed to melt three different kitchenware items in the oven. She remained calm, cool and collected, while I was having a meltdown myself! Her zest for life is amazing, as is her desire for peace in our world and in our own individual hearts. She has, and will always be an inspiration to me.

Comments for Marie's Book ①

Marie and I have been friends for forty-five years, and we have seen each other through many of life's wonderful events. When my first daughter, Rachel was born, Marie was there to hold her close. Then when my second daughter, Rebecca, was a toddler, she asked, Marie, if she could sit on her lap. Recently, when Marie was visiting, Rebecca's oldest son asked her if he could sit on her lap. They could sense her wonderful loving energy, and were all drawn to her. Both of my daughters and all of my six small grandchildren feel a special connection to Marie and enjoy being around her.

Marie is one of the most amazing people I have ever known. She is so talented in so many worldly ways, yet she is so able to share and create a very lovely healing presence to all. Her beautiful harp music has had a wonderful, soothing and healing effect on so many patients in the hospital setting. And now, she is also playing the piano to others in need of comfort and healing.

Marie always reminds me of what having a sense of gratitude really means. She has an everpresent sense of gratitude to all around her, as well as for all of life's daily experiences that come her way. She sets an amazing example for all of us. I have always felt so lucky to have Marie as a friend.

Anne McAliffe
Palo Alto, California

Del: Masters degree in Accounting from Texas University.
Ist Lt. in Regensburg, Germany for three years.
Texaco Chemical Sales Sr. Rep. for West Coast for 30 years.

Marie: Grail Lay Mission work in U.S. & 7 years in Indonesia.
Masters degree in Socio-Linguistics from Stanford University.
Taught Indonesian Language at Stanford for 10 years.
Indonesian Language Interpreter for U.S. Department of State since 1981.
Author and translator of several books.

18011 North Timber Ridge Drive
Surprise, Arizona 85374:
Phone: 623-214-2406

"For all that has been Thanks.
To all that shall be Yes"
Dag Hammersjold

Thoughts of Marie -   *Gregg*

I've known Marie for many years, and first had the pleasure of meeting her in Arizona in the early 2000's at a Stanford Alumni Association faculty guest speaker brunch. As president of the Phoenix Chapter of the alumni association, I was introduced to Marie, and I immediately recognized the name 'Grandstaff' as being the maiden name of Kathryn Crosby, widow of Bing Crosby, who lived near me as I grew up on the San Francisco peninsula. I asked Marie if there was by chance any connection, and she said "Yes, Kathryn's brother is Del - my husband." I'd known Kathryn Crosby had one sister and one brother, and Marie was the wife of Del. It was terrific meeting Marie that day, and she had an effervescence that sort of lit up the banquet room at the hotel where the Stanford event was being held.

After that first meeting, Marie and I saw each other at future Stanford events. We lived just minutes from each other, so we would see each other at gatherings at her home or mine. I remember going to harp concerts / big and small - at Marie's house. I remember another time ~~her~~ doctor *[Dr. Pozu, her Cardiologist]* and friend played a trumpet and Marie played her grand piano *and harp*. We attended more Stanford events and had lots of fun.

When I moved back to California from Arizona, it was fun to see Marie every time she came to San Francisco to see her family and friends. I enjoyed lunches and any possible activity where we could enjoy some time spent visiting. This week, Marie is ~~in town and we had drinks~~ at Kathryn Crosby's home ~~after picking Marie up at the airport~~. My ~~friends Sonya and Bob came along and we had a terrific time~~. Marie was headed out later to see Beach Blanket Babylon in the City with Kathryn and other friends.

Saturday night Marie will be the guest of honor at a dinner in Palo Alto, and I'm looking forward to seeing her there - at the home of friends Ann and Tim. Sunday Marie will accompany me to my church - St. Matthews' Episcopal - in San Mateo.

I'm lucky to have met Marie. We have shared good times - and helped each other through some trying times as well. Nobody could have done more to help cheer me up during a brief low period I went through several years ago. And I hope I helped keep Marie's spirits up when she went through a serious health crisis as well. She looks absolutely terrific again - and when I picked her up at the airport a few days ago, I couldn't believe how youthful, joyous and content Marie looked. And she was wearing a bright and wide smile! It is such a pleasure seeing Marie every chance we get. I look forward to many more times. I think of Marie as my "sister" and I'm happy to say she gives me the honorary title of her "brother" as well.

Gregg Rathbarn   *San Jose, CA*

Subj: **my thoughts of Marie Grandstaff**
Date: 6/7/2013 1:33:53 P.M. US Mountain Standard Time
From: MEsber7855@aol.com
         llewhowell8@gmail.com
To:

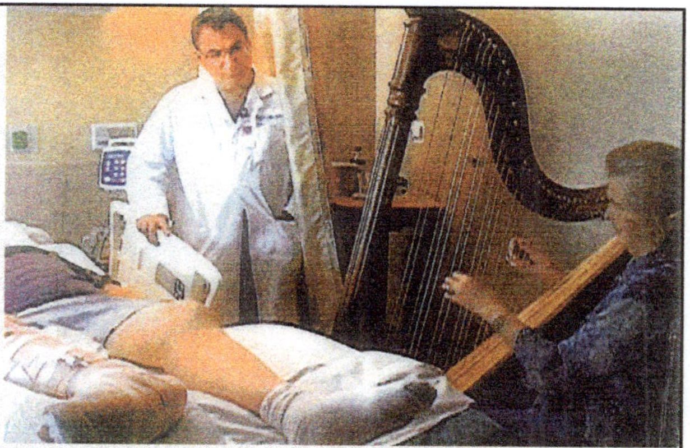

Michael F. Esber, DPM, PC
Arizona Foot Health Center
14300 Granite Valley Dr.
Suite # 5-B
Sun City West, AZ 85375
Phone: (623) 546-4930
E-mail: mesber7855@aol.com

I met Maria Grandstaff (AKA Maria Louisa) of course to me only) a couple of years ago at Del Webb Hospital. She played the harp for one of my patients Doug. Her song was angelic. She had her usual smile that starts wide, followed by twitches of bigger smiles with intermittent eye blinks. Her music was angelic and her presence was very reassuring. Since that day Maria and I have become very close friends. My kids love her and call her Auntie Marie.

Maria is kind and thoughtful. She doesn't miss a birthday or an event without the appropriate card or gift. Maria is a true encyclopedia with a sharp memory. She remembers names of people past even if she met them only once. ███ █████████ happened yesterday. Maria remembers old events and incidents like it ███ ██████. She is a very caring individual who showers you with plenty of hugs, a touch of her hand, a bundle of smiles and beautiful eyes that smothers you with love and affection. Maria is very intelligent and well versed on many subjects including politics, religion, art and especially music. She is not afraid to voice her opinion and most people pause when she speaks and listen to her words of wisdom. ██ ██████████████████████████████████. Maria Louisa is a wise mentor and reliable source of knowledge. Most of all she is a great friend that you can always count on. "Go Maria".

Michael Esber

Marie's Journey of Love

Addendums
Part II. Articles, Honors, and Letters

Grandpa and Grandma Mohr

The More Mohrs, the Merrier!
18 Plus Get Back Home to Pete, Anna

ST. MARK, Kan.— It isn't often that all children of Peter and Anna Mohr are able to get home at the same time. When they do, it's a convention.

For the first time in nine years all 18 Mohr children gathered at the family homestead in this farming community northwest of Wichita. Some of them came from as far away as Germany.

With tear-brimmed eyes, Anna Mohr said: "When they were growing up, we didn't see how we could have been happier. But we are happier now with all back with us again."

Pete Mohr, a farmer, agreed. "We are proud of them. They have turned out well."

THE MOHRS are six girls and 12 boys. The eldest is Sr. Mary Denise, a Benedictine, who teaches at Christ the King school in Oklahoma City. Fr. Boniface Mohr, also a Benedictine, teaches at St. Gregory's high school in Shawnee, Okla. He offered his first solemn Mass at this year's reunion.

Mike Mohr, who served in the Pacific in World War II, is now a farmer, father of three boys and a girl. Nick Mohr, who served in Germany in World War II, is a machinist, father of four boys and two girls.

William was in the Korean conflict. Clarence and John Mohr were mustered out of the army after serving in Germany.

Through a special request of U.S. Sen. Mike Monoiney of Oklahoma, Pete and Anthony Mohr, serving with the army in Germany, were granted leave to come home for the reunion.

Clarence, John and Bart Mohr attend St. Gregory's college in Shawnee, Greg Mohr goes to St. Gregory's high school there.

Marie, second-oldest daughter, is employed at the Grail Overseas institute in Brooklyn, N.Y. The institute prepares American women to serve overseas as lay Catholic missioners. Theresa attends Sacred Heart college in Wichita.

Still at home are Josephine Ann, William, Al, Francis and Margaret, who attend school and help out with chores around the farm and house.

Pete Mohr, a farmer all his life, can attest his "harvest" has been good.

Inside Your Michigan Catholic

Book Reviews	8
Bible and You	4
Editorial	4
Family Life Events	8
Here's the Answer	4
Missions	8
Movie Guide	10
Real Estate Guide	11
Sports	6
TV-Movie Guide	12
TV-Radio Guide	11
Want Ads	11
Women's News	9
Youth Pages	7

Feb 5, 1959 — Michigan Catholic

Marie's Journey of Love

KNIGHT OF THE GOOD EARTH

Michael Mohr, the only U.S. farmer made Knight of St. Gregory.

MIKE MOHR of St. Mark's, Kansas, has the enviable distinction of being the first and the only farmer in the United States to be made a Knight of St. Gregory. Perhaps I should not say "farmer." Sir Michael Mohr is more than a farmer; he is an aristocrat of the soil. But he has known hardships and privations. He could tell you how much went into the life of the Kansas prairie pioneer of fifty years ago.

Mike's career stretches out over a period of 75 years, beginning in quaint Nattenheim, Germany, where he was born. His father was a "gross" farmer. He owned one hundred acres of land, which is considered a "gross" or big farm in Germany even today. But big farmer Mohr also had a big family, 15 children, of which Mike was the oldest.

The one hundred acres were none too many; they supported the big family well enough but did not make it possible for the parents to lay by very much for the rainy day. Moreover, if the one hundred acres were equally divided among the children, there would be scarcely seven acres for each child. Seven acres is not exactly a princely inheritance. So Mike decided that the sensible thing to do would be to go to America and get a hundred acres for himself.

Then, too, by leaving home he would lessen the burden his father was carrying. One child less at home would decrease the family overhead. And another thing: Mike did not like the military spirit in Germany. After having served his time in the army, he had returned home thoroughly disgusted with the Prussian military regime that delighted in army maneuvers and in the sound of marching hob-nailed boots and the rattling of sabers. He definitely didn't like war. It was in the cards that in the event of war, Mike would have to serve. In America, he knew, there was no military compulsion. It was a country where freedom and liberty flourished —and opportunities were many. Western America was being settled. His uncle, Bartel Betzen, who had immigrated to America in 1880, had written many letters in which he gave a glowing account of the new country.

Mike reasoned: Suppose he were to have luck in America? Why, a hundred acres of land was not out of the question. Think of it—in a few years he might be the owner of as much land as his father, aided by an inheritance from his grandfather, had succeeded in accumulating in a long lifetime.

Mike set foot on American soil in New York City, on December 23, 1892. All he had in the world was the price of a railroad ticket to Kansas, a little bundle of cloth nd a burning, hopeful ambition. He spent the greater part of his first American Christmas in Chicago's Dearborn railway station, somewhat homesick and lonesome. At home, he knew, there would be, oh! so many good things—for in dear old Nattenheim Christmas was celebrated in truly wondrous fashion.

As the train bore Mike west, his spirits drooped still more. Kansas!, My, what a hungry-looking country it was, without forests, good roads, big cities, or snug, pretty little villages. There were occasional stretches of plowed ground. What wheat he saw was sickly, looking for want of moisture. There had been a long drought, and the winter snows had been only flurries. Whatever in the world made uncle

As long as men have the vision, grit and hardihood of Mike Mohr, America will be worth fighting for

FEBRUARY, 1945

128

He attended many legislature sessions at Topeka, learned the lay-of-the-land and the way of the politicians, stormed to the front whenever he heard of a proposed piece of legislation that was unfavorable to the farmer's interests, and helped to head off the iniquitous thing.

He interested himself in the cooperative movement. He engineered the buying of a elevator at Colwich, Kansas, by a group of farmers, to bring into existence the Farmers Cooperative Elevator. Mike has been president of this concern since 1915, and has helped to make it pay fat dividends a good many years. He was also instrumental in establishing two other coöp elevators in the vicinity of Saint Mark's.

The same driving interest in things agricultural that make Mike Mohr a progressive farmer has characterized his Catholic life. The Catholic parochial school system has never had a more staunch supporter than Mike. To this day, he fetches a car load of his grandchildren—there are 43 altogether—to the parish school every day. "This daily chore," he says, "helps to keep me young and parish-school-minded."

For many years Mike served the interests of his parish as a member of the church committee. But it was as a leader in the work of the Catholic Central Verein of America that Mike came to be known beyond the state of Kansas. For almost forty years he has been a superb Central Vereiner and has regularly attended conventions all over the country, oftentimes booked as a speaker on the program, and always in the thick of floor discussions. The name "Mike Mohr" is a household word wherever the Central Verein exists. He was president of the Kansas Branch of this society for eighteen consecutive years, is a trustee at the present time.

Of course this sort of success-climbing is nothing unusual in free and fabulous America. Many immigrants have reached high ground by climbing laboriously, doggedly, painstakingly. But it so happens that Mike's Bishop, the Most Rev. Christian H. Winkelmann, of Wichita, has a splendid weakness that runs to idolizing a Horatio Alger career cast from a Catholic mold. I mention this because it is the circumstance in Mike Mohr's life which is responsible for his being raised to a rank no other immigrant in rural America has ever reached.

So the Bishop sent a brief account of this Catholic Kansan to the Holy Father. And not long after the Pope graciously conferred the Knighthood of St. Gregory on Michael Mohr. He was invested at the Cathedral, in Wichita, on September 10, 1943.

FEBRUARY, 1945   —1943—

ORDEN SOBERANA DE CABALLEROS MEDICOS
DE SAN JUAN DE JERUSALEN
SOVEREIGN MEDICAL ORDER OF THE KNIGHTS HOSPITALLER
SAINT JOHN OF JERUSALEM

This is to certify that

Marie Mohr-Grandstaff

has record for exceptional performance to contribute and render public and community health, contributing to our Monastic Hospital Foundations and to world good, the Sovereign Council hereby bestows upon the above named, the designation of

Dame of Honour

July 12th, 2008
Phoenix, Arizona USA

His Excellency, Prof. Charles McWilliams
Grand Master

Honorary Degree

Conferred on

Gregory Mohr

in
Agriculture ~ Farming ~ Gardening

for
Outstanding Achievements
and years of dedicated service
to the
Mohr Family Partnership

To our beloved brother
Gregory Mohr
on this day of

Thanksgiving ~ *November 2007*

From his grateful and loving brothers and sisters

FIRST TO GO FROM DIOCESE
Wichita Woman To Be Missioner

Wichita.—The first lay missionary from the Wichita Diocese is preparing to leave for Indonesia in the near future.

Marie Mohr, daughter of Peter and Anna Mohr of St. Mark's, is home for a visit from Ohio and New York, where she has been working with the Grail for 10 years. In the latter part of June she will return to New York to complete her training course, and then in early September she will leave for East Java, Surabaja, Indonesia.

Miss Mohr said that Bishop Mark K. Carroll, who came to visit her family last week, gave his wholehearted encouragement and stressed the importance of the lay person's assuming his responsibility as an apostle and follower of Christ.

International Team

In Java she will be working with a team composed of a Chinese girl and a woman from Holland, who are already there, and a Philippine girl, now at Grailville in Ohio, who will accompany her to the mission.

They will work in the diocese of Bishop Klooster.

For specific training, Miss Mohr has participated in an eight-month training program for overseas service in Brooklyn, N. Y. Father Edward Murphy, S. J., Father Considine, M. M., and others contributed to the program, which included such studies as missionology, area studies, importance of prayer and spiritual deepening, and other practical preparations

She also obtained a bachelor of science degree in general home economics.

Previously she had served two years at the training center in Ohio and was a staff member at the International Student Center in New York for four years and a student and staff member at Grail Overseas Institute in Brooklyn for four years.

"The Grail," she explained, "is an international movement in the lay apostolate that brings together young women of all nations and races, who strive to work out concretely the Christian ideal in fields as family life, community building, pro-
(Turn to Page 2 — Column 1)

Beginning of Trend Bishop Mark K. Carroll greets Marie Mohr of St. Mark's on her visit home before leaving for the missions in Indonesia. Miss Mohr, who has been in Grail work in Ohio and New York, is the first lay missionary from the Wichita Diocese to go to the foreign missions, Bishop Carroll stated. "I hope this is the beginning of a trend in our diocese. The Church is eager to have the lay people take up the apostolate."

Lay Missionary of St. Mark Parish Will Go to Indonesia

A young rural Wichita woman will leave this country for Indonesia in September to become the first Catholic lay missionary from the Wichita diocese.

Marie Mohr, daughter of Mr. and Mrs. Peter Mohr in St. Mark parish, is going to East Java, Surabaja, Indonesia. She and a team of other young women trained for the work will establish a residence for young women attending a university there.

Miss Mohr said the residence is patterned on similar lines to a sorority house. Purpose of the training center, as it is called, is to develop a sense of responsibility in students and encourage them to develop their talents and standards.

Miss Mohr graduated from Grailville Community College in Ohio, where she majored in home economics and lay religious training.

International Plan

Grail is an international movement in the lay apostolate that brings together young women from over the world to work in Christian endeavors, she said.

Since her graduation from Grailville Community College, she has been working with the movement at International Youth Center, New York City.

This work, she said, sparked her enthusiasm for overseas mission work. She found meeting with young persons from other countries interesting and decided to go into the program more deeply.

She recently completed an eight-month training program

FABRIC EXPLAINED—The intricate process of making batik, a hand-made, hand-printed Far Eastern fabric, is explained by Marie Mohr for her parents, Mr. and Mrs. Peter Mohr, rural Wichita. Miss Mohr will travel to Indonesia in September to be the first Catholic lay missionary from the Wichita diocese. — (Eagle Staff Photo.)

given by Grail in Brooklyn, N.Y. She left Wichita Thursday night to return to New York City, where she will take two education courses at New York University.

She will be away from the United States at least five years, which is the minimum amount of time one must spend on a mission of this sort, she added.

Marie's Journey of Love

Marie Mohr of St. Marks Bound Soon for Indonesia

St. Marks — Marie Mohr, daughter of Mr. and Mrs. Peter Mohr of St. Mark's parish here, a Grail worker in Indonesia, has returned home after a summer Catechetical Institute at Grailville, Loveland, O.

Miss Mohr, who left for Indonesia in 1960 as a lay mission worker, will soon be returning to the nation known as the "land of the Three Thousand Islands."

The "figure is not an exaggeration," she said. "About 2,-00 of them are inhabited."

WHEN INDONESIA gained Independence in 1949, President Achmed Sukarno proclaimed the five fundamental principles on which the new state would be based. They are belief in God, belief in man, belief in the Indonesian nation, belief in the sovereignty of the nation, and belief in social justice.

"It is generally said that Indonesia is 90 per cent Islamic but the country is not an Islamic state."

It has a total population of about one hundred million.

"These principles represent the spirit of the Indonesian people and are in full harmony with Christian social principles," Miss Mohr said.

"Just shortly after my arrival in Indonesia three years ago," she continued, "the ecclesiastical heirarchy was established. There are now six archdioceses and 19 dioceses, two vicariates, and three prefectures apostolic.

"The most active group of Catholics are on the island of Flores. The most influential, however, are the Catholics in Java. Whatever the future holds in store for the country, the faith is solidly established."

Miss Mohr noted there is Catholic influence in the armed forces, which are strongly set against Communism, a great threat there."

THE GOVERNMENT allots funds for a program of training about 3,000 students. There are 77 hospitals and 159 out-patient clinics.

"The Sodality is well organized and, in East Java, Legion of Mary groups are active," Miss Mohr commented.

"I HAVE BEEN in East Java as the leader of our Grail team. There we have been active in catechetical work giving introductory programs on the apostolate and liturgy. We are trying to build up a library and reading-meeting room for the people of Surabaja.

"Thus in a Catholic population of about 1,500,000, or about one and one half percent of the total population. There are only 200 native priests among the 1200 laboring there and approximately 900 native nuns among 2,400.

"The Church has at the moment 2,009 elementary schools, 474 secondary schools and one Catholic university which has dent Sukarno, in trying to build up a country with so many varying elements, is anxious to assure all the people the right of religious freedom," she added.

"The history of Indonesian Catholicism," she pointed out, "belongs to both the distant past and recent times.

"If we are quick and alert and capture the tremendous opportunity open to us now in Indonesia, the once long ago dream of St. Francis Xavier will truly be realized," Miss Mohr said in concluding. "For now as never before can we say with St. Francis that "Indonesia is the Island of Hope.""

In Indonesia

With two Indonesian university students who live at the Grail Center in Indonesia where they take part in the activities and programs of the Grail movement in Marie Mohr, daughter of Mr. and Mrs. Peter Mohr of St. Mark's parish, St. Mark's, a Grail worker in Indonesia who is on leave at home after three years mission work.

Important article Marie to Indonesia

Advance Register
Friday, April 28, 1961

Lay Missioner Writes
Letter From Indonesia

Wichita. — Exotic beauty and hope for the future is told in the first newsletter from Marie Mohr, lay missioner from St. Marks, Kan., who traveled to Indonesia last winter to work with the Grail.

Following is the letter in part:

Dear Friends,

From the paradise-like land of the Far East, Indonesia, come our warm greetings and love to each of you. Though oceans and countries separate us, still we trust that the coming years will continue to be this joint endeavor with the continued support of your prayers and encouragement.

The weeks spent at our International Center in Holland were valuable ones. Our unity with young women from all parts of the world was very tangible. One evening a group of 12 had casually gathered for a discussion, and we realized that we were all from a different country. Some of our members who had just returned from the Congo were there to share the recent happenings in that country.

The week in Rome was wonderful. One feels very near to the early Christian here. Everywhere we felt urged to beg Our Lord for that same strength of soul and conviction of heart which characterized the lives of the early Christian heroes. We felt privileged to be present for one of the semiprivate audiences of our Holy Father. We heard from his own lips his one recurring plea for *unity* among all people.

Each quick, short stop in Karachi, Calcutta, Bangkok and Singapore introduced us farther into the atmosphere of the Orient.

At 12 midnight, Nov 16, the stewardess announced, "Fasten your seat belts; we are preparing to land." This was exactly the ninth time we were hearing these words in the past months, but this time it caused a completely new sensation. It was the end and the beginning in one eventful moment; the end of our long journey and the beginning of our new task!

ORIENTATION

After a day in Djakarta we traveled to Semarang where we have spent these first three months of orientation. Being in Central Java gives us the opportunity to learn about the Javanese culture. Immediately we began our language class and have already had some good healthy laughs about our mistakes.

The country of Indonesia is truly beautiful. We drove to a lovely spot in the mountains one day for some time of quiet. Here we had time to sit and drink in the beauty of the surrounding area. On one side lay the ingeniously terraced rice "sawahs" rising like an immense hill of steps leading up, up and up. Majestic and quiet, it seemed to invite one to ascend the altar of the planet earth, set in the midst of God's temple, the Cosmos.

We have arrived here during a very historical moment of development in the life of the Church in Indonesia. The Holy Father has just granted the title of diocese to all vicariates here. We now have six Archbishops; three of these are indigenous. Other signs of new life are evident. We attended a High Mass where the singing was accompanied by the "gamelan," another High Mass where the entire congregation sang the responses. There are many conversions among the young people.

With a moderate knowledge of the language and a variety of introduction to the atmosphere and life here, I find myself preparing to leave for Surabaja on April 1, where we begin more specifically our task in Indonesia. As a student here I shall begin my research study on "Culture and Customs in the Indonesian Family." Through this study there will be the opportunity to make contacts with students and families which are a very necessary step for the growth and development of the work at this time.

We hope this letter reaches you in time to bring you our Easter wishes, or as we say here "SELAMAT HARI PASCHA!"

Yours in Christ,
Marie Mohr

135

Marie's Journey of Love

Off to Indonesia — Arriving shortly in Central Java, Indonesia, will be Miss Marie Mohr, right, daughter of Mr. and Mrs. Pete Mohr, St. Mark's, and Baidy Mendoza, seated, center, of the Philippines. The two are shown above at a farewell party given for them recently at the Brooklyn Grail Center. Others, left to right, are Elizabeth Namaganda, Uganda; Aida Sequera, Bombay, India; and Arlene Chen, Hong Kong.

St. Mark's Girl to Found Indonesian Grail Center

Brooklyn, N.Y.—Arriving at Semarang, Indonesia, this month will be two young women of the Grail Movement. Marie Mohr, daughter of Mr. and Mrs. Pete Mohr of St. Mark's, and Baidy Mendoza of the Philippines are joining international Grail teams already at work in Surabaja, Semarang, and Bogor.

The special assignment of the two young women will be the establishment of a Grail Center in Central Java for community development programs among Indonesian women and girls.

Miss Mohr is a graduate of Pratt Institute and is a home economist. For some years she has served on the staff of the Grail Institute for Overseas Service in Brooklyn. Miss Mendoza worked four years among the tribal people of Borneo.

During the past year 15 Grail members from the United States were assigned to posts in South Africa, Ghana, Uganda, Vietnam, and Brazil. As doctors, nurses, teachers, secretaries, home economists, they are devoting themselves to the spiritual and human welfare of the people they go to serve.

A team of seven young women currently are in training at the Grail Overseas Service center, 308 Clinton Avenue, Brooklyn, preparing for assignments in Latin America. The training lasts one year and afterward the team is sent, on a contract basis, for a period of three years. A new group will be admitted to the training on March 1, 1961.

International Grail Work Much Like Peace Corps

It's time for America to restore the meaning to such words as freedom, democracy and love, Maria Virginia Mohr, a worker in the International Grail movement, told Monte Cassino students Tuesday. Miss Mohr talked to elementary and high school students at two special assemblies held so she could discuss what the Grail movement is and what it is doing around the world.

She is the sister of Mother Marie Denise, superior of the Benedictine Sisters of St. Joseph's Convent in Tulsa.

The movement started in Holland in 1912 and now has spread to include women of five continents.

"We are not sisters," said Miss Mohr, "but lay apostles who stay

Photo on Page 1, Sec. 2

in whatever work we pursue." She has been living the past three years in Indonesia, teaching English at the university located in the capital city of Surabaja on the Island of Java.

A close personal friend of the late Dr. Tom Dooley, Miss Mohr said Indonesia literacy has risen from 7 to 70 per cent since 1940. There are 3,000 islands comprising Indonesia, she said, but only 2,000 are inhabited. The population is about 100 million.

"About 1.5 per cent of the people are Catholic," she said, "another 3.5 per cent are Protestant, and nearly 90 per cent of Islamic faith.

"The people speak about 100 different languages, but since 1921 one basic language has grown up from a Malayan root."

Her work is similar to that done by Peace Corps members in that she lives with the people and shares what they have.

"We try to become a part of their cultural way of life," said Miss Mohr, "and we do this by living with them and learning more about them."

Miss Mohr said there is strong Christian leadership in Indonesia, but she added Communism is a definite threat to the nation.

She is en route to Indonesia to begin another tour of duty, but first she will travel to Europe for two weeks of workshop in Paris. She then will visit Rome and the Middle East before returning to Indonesia.

Her audiences Tuesday included not only Monte Cassino students but also members of the Benedictine community in Tulsa.

Puppets Part of a Culture
A sacred leather puppet was among Indonesian articles brought to Tulsa Tuesday by Marie Virginia Mohr who has spent three years there teaching English to university students. The puppets are operated from below a stage and are used for shows. Examining the puppets are Mother Marie Denise, sister of Miss Mohr, and a second grade student, Jerry McGrann, son of Mr. and Mrs. Roy T. McGrann, of 2231 S. Delaware Place. A colorful piece of cloth brought back by the worker in the Grail movement was shown as an example of how the Indonesians dye their material. (Story on Page 8.)

24—PALO ALTO TIMES, PALO ALTO, CALIF., THURSDAY, OCT. 26, 1972

Sounds of Indonesia

Jeanne Blamey, a political science student, tries pronouncing words written by teacher Marie Mohr as graduate student Michael Dove ponders the pronounciation.

Some unusual languages in classes at Stanford

Most college alumni remember grappling with French, German or one of the other European languages which are standard offerings on college curriculum.

But Stanford University students can also try their hand at Twi, Amharic, and several other less well-known tongues.

Besides courses in French, Spanish, Italian, German, Russian, Chinese, Portuguese, classical Latin, Greek and Japanese, Stanford offers 12 other languages.

All this came about through the efforts of the Interdisciplinary Committee on Linguistics, chaired by Prof. Charles A. Ferguson.

Average class size is eight to 10 students. Almost 100 students are in the program.

There are several one-student courses, including Amharic, the language of Ethiopia, and modern Greek. These involve graduate students who plan more research in the language of the country.

There are also two courses in Twi (pronounced "swee"), the language of Ghana.

"At the request of any student," Ferguson said, "we will set up a language program even if there's only one student provided he has a legitimate academic reason for needing the language, and provided we can find a competent instructor to teach it."

The program coordinator is Jame Duran, a doctoral candidate in linguistic from San Jose.

Among the language choices are elementary and intermediate Hebrew Latvian and Norwegian, as well as elementary Yiddish, Indonesian, and Irish Gaelic.

Also available are classes in Czech and modern Arabic, as well as a special tutoring program for American Indian under the direction of Gil DeLisle.

"The program is experimental," Ferguson noted, "but even with limited funds, the student response has been enthusiastic."

Students interested in organizing a specialized language course for 1973-74 may visit the linguistics office in Building 100, Inner Quad, to fill out an application

Marie's Journey of Love

Marie with Lesa Caldarella-Wong, poet, author, and friend

sweet sacrifice

so much of who we really are as people
the goodness and realness of what we are made of
is what is left of us as we get older

it is like we cannot
hide anymore behind our words and fears
everything just sifts down

our true selves
are revealed with age

our actions, our words,
expose our souls
we can only be who we are

the veil and skin becomes
transparent with age

if we are happy people
then we will love

if we are generous
than we will be giving

if we are humble
then we are able to forgive

if we are that sweet sacrifice
then we shall see god

by Lesa Caldarella-Wong
© copy write protected

About the Author

Marie Mohr-Grandstaff, from a family of eighteen children, hails from the small farm community of Wichita, Kansas. She launched her career by working for the International Grail Women's Movement. For seven years, she lived overseas teaching English and Religion in Indonesia and became an expert in the culture and language. After she left her post with Grail, Marie took on a four-month assignment as a guest lecturer on a cruise ship that sailed to many countries in Southeast Asia.

Marie's mastery of language and culture led her to a teaching position at Stanford University, where she taught the Indonesian language for ten years. She capped off her accomplished career with a prestigious assignment with the U.S. State Department as an Indonesian language interpreter and translator in the USA and in Indonesia.

Marie attended the Pratt Institute and New York University, and she earned a bachelor's degree. She also holds a master's degree in socio-linguistics from Stanford University.

Marie is multilingual—in English, German, and Indonesian. She is an author, lecturer, and translator of several books. Her writing is greatly influenced by her close-knit family upbringing, travel, teaching, spirituality, love for her late husband Del, family, friends, and appreciation for music.

She is a gifted pianist and harpist, and serves as a "living medicine ionary" on the advisory board of the Harp Foundation in Phoenix. ves in Surprise, Arizona and is active with the Grail, as well as c and cultural causes. Her most recent book, *Marie's Journey* e story of her life.